SUPER-PETS & SMART OWNERS

To Andy and Emma
with love and affection

SUPER-PETS
&
SMART OWNERS

The Care of Familiar and Unfamiliar Creatures

by
MIKE MOORE

PARAPRESS
LIMITED
TUNBRIDGE WELLS

Also published by Parapress:
Your First Great Dane by Angela Mitchell

ISBN: 1-898594-74-0

First published in the UK by
PARAPRESS LTD
5 Bentham Hill House
Stockland Green Road
Tunbridge Wells
Kent TN3 0TJ
www.parapress.co.uk

A catalogue record for this book is available
from the British Library

Typeset in 11 on 13pt Rotis Sans Serif by
Vitaset, Paddock Wood, Kent

Printed in Great Britain by
Biddles Ltd, Guildford & Kings Lynn

ACKNOWLEDGEMENTS

A big thank you to Pamela L. West of Henderson, Nevada, for her generous help with information on pricing and other conditions in the United States; also to Bill Wright for kindly allowing me the free use of his animal photos, and to Kevin Kelland for his picture of me.

Mike Moore

CONTENTS

1
INTRODUCTION

THE KEEPING OF ANIMALS

This book aims to be comprehensively informative about animals which are kept as pets, or in semi-captivity. Many of these animals have been our companions for decades, centuries, or even millennia. During the past few years, however, there has been a growing tendency for people to acquire more exotic creatures. The rabbit and the canary, for example, have been overtaken in popularity by the monkey and the parrot.

Exotic creatures are, by definition, those with which people in western society are less familiar. The understanding of their care and management is, therefore, becoming of greater concern, since owners may not have enough knowledge or experience available to them.

Long-billed Corella parrot

We need to think carefully about keeping animals in captivity, and about the consequences, both for ourselves and for them. In many books written on the care of certain exotic pets, some important matters tend to be overlooked, such as the running costs of keeping them, which can be a lot higher than a purchaser expects (as an example, the cost of keeping a small monkey in proper condition is given below).

This book takes a positive view of pet ownership, believing that it plays a genuinely important role in the lives of humans and animals alike. It tries to give an overall picture of what to look for when obtaining a pet, so that a healthy animal is always obtained. Caging animals (if necessary), heating and lighting (where necessary), diets, breeding, and general care and management are covered throughout the book. A comprehensive feeding appendix outlines food chemicals, natural and artificial foodstuffs, substitute foods and supplements.

A General Reference section gives an A–Z of those animals which are available from bona fide pet dealers and good professional pet shops.

Finally, there are sections at the back of the book on hygiene and disease, pests and parasites, animal first aid and useful addresses.

THE REAL COSTS

All prices in this book were correct at the time of printing, but are subject to change, so treat them as a rough guide. Prices are in UK sterling and US dollars.

A small monkey can cost between £150 and £350 ($220–510) to purchase, but, when looking at the proper caging for such an animal, a further £100 ($145) plus may be needed. Lighting and heating can cost a further £50 ($73) plus per year. Then there is the cost of the feeding.

Fruit prices vary during the year, and monkeys will only eat fresh fruit, so obtaining bruised and half rotten fruit is really a false economy as most will be thrown away. Think of the animal in the wild, and what fruit it would take from its natural environment: the best.

Brown bread can also be given, as not only does this provide a source of roughage for the animal, but it will enjoy it. Most monkeys and some other small mammals eat many insects, such as crickets, locusts and mealworms. The price of these vary, but can cost a further £2-£3 ($3- 4.50) per week, depending on the number of animals kept.

Pygmy Marmoset

Some foodstuffs that are imported lack trace elements, e.g. those that would be found on the skins of fruits, but adding a mineral supplement which is normally purchased in powder form can put back these trace elements into the diet. Extra vitamins have also to be added, especially D3, the sunshine vitamin, which helps to guard against bone deformities in primates. Vitamin and mineral powders are not very expensive, around £3 ($4.50) per tub, which should last about three months, again depending on the number of animals.

WHY KEEP ANIMALS IN THE FIRST PLACE?

First of all we have to ask ourselves, do we really want to keep animals in captivity? The answer to this is obvious to those people who are animal lovers and want to learn more about them and, more importantly, to have animals in close proximity to themselves as part of the family.

Then there are others who say that the act of incarcerating creatures for our own satisfaction and enjoyment is immoral and obscene, and takes us back to the Victorian times when this sort of practice was considered commonplace.

Others point to the trade in wild creatures which can lead to cruelty and to endangering their existence.

All these arguments are valid to some extent, and it is not the purpose of this book to condone any form of abuse or exploitation. Rather it is to help provide knowledge in a field which seems inevitably set to expand.

RESTORING THE WILD

The world as we know it can be considered as left us in trust by our ancestors, for us to look after and to pass on to the next generation. Unfortunately, much of the earth is being increasingly exploited, and many species of animals, plants, and other life forms are disappearing at a formidable rate.

Food chains and food webs are the main structures of the animal kingdom, each part relying on the next and so on. As soon as these parts begin to break down by a form of animal or plant life disappearing, then other animals begin to suffer from it. Although it is true that over millennia species have always become extinct, this process has formerly been complemented by the evolution of new species. This evolution takes time, and cannot function to maintain the variety of life if the rate of extinction becomes too fast.

Meerkat

As a zoologist I can understand the objectives of keeping animals in captivity to maintain the species. That is to say that as long as people want to keep animals, they will be bred for that reason. This in turn prevents the further depletion of stocks in the wild. The Red-kneed Tarantula from Mexico has always been a fascinating favourite with American children, in fact some 85% of them have owned one, and not so long ago the trend also began in the UK. Because of the great demand for this creature, the stocks in the wild began to decrease so badly that there was great concern that it would eventually die out. The Mexican government finally closed the door to any more being taken from the wild, which led to some specialist zoos, and private invertebrate keepers beginning to breed them solely for the pet trade. This has been a very successful exercise, and the remaining wild stocks are now beginning to increase.

The lemurs of Madagascar have suffered massive habitat loss, and numbers in the little forest that remains are heavily depleted. All species are now protected, and in Britain are to be found only in specialist zoos.

There is another factor in the debate, and that is the breeding of rare and endangered species for human food, so that those species do not go into extinction. This has already begun in various parts of Africa, where some of the rarer species of antelope are being intensively bred for food, and the wild stocks are now improving and should be saved from further decline. The ostrich is another animal that is now farmed and successfully bred for the table, becoming very popular food, as other birds have in the past.

Kudu

With man's interference in nature as a whole, including deforestation, pollution, wanton cruelty, and the greenhouse effect as examples, the habitats of some of our more exotic species are disappearing at an alarming rate, along with the animals themselves. At the end of the twentieth century, two new species of marmoset were discovered from the basin of Rio Madeira, in the state of Amazonas, Brazil. Undoubtedly this was a remarkable discovery, but how many unknown species of animal have disappeared off our earth without any knowledge of their existence? It is something we shall never know.

What has been learned over the years, by keeping animals in captivity, is now gradually being put to use in the wild state, where several species have been saved from extinction through this ongoing knowledge.

The Hawaiian Goose, or Ne-Ne, was taken into captivity by Sir Peter Scott at the Slimbridge Wildfowl Trust, now known as the Wetlands and Wildfowl Trust, when their numbers became depleted in the wild. The birds eventually began to breed and many were reintroduced into Hawaii and the surrounding islands, where they have successfully maintained their existence.

Ne-Ne goose

The Golden-lion Tamarin, a small monkey from Brazil, diminished to just a few specimens in the wild. One of the reasons for this decline was the taking of their silky golden furred skins by the local people, for the elaborate decorations on many of the costumes for the Mardi Gras, that takes place each year. With permission from the Brazilian Government in the 1980s, animals were taken from different areas of the Brazilian rain forest by one of the major zoos in the United States of America.

These selected animals were sexually partnered as potential breeding pairs, and placed into captivity on what is zoologically known as a 'captive breeding programme'. Governed by a studbook listing all the individuals, their date of capture, their sexes, estimated age, identity number, etc., these 'guinea pigs' soon became accustomed to a captive environment and subsequently began to breed. The resulting offspring were entered into the studbook, and a few of the world's better zoos were approached, to help in the maintenance and further breeding of this animal. At the same time, a careful watch was kept on them by the studbook keeper, to prevent any interbreeding.

Since that time, many of the offspring have been successfully re-introduced into the wild, where they have taken their place within the rain forest canopies, and are now breeding in their own right. Their numbers are beginning to intensify, so much so that it is only necessary to breed a small quantity in captivity, just to 'top up' the numbers in the wild every so often. All Golden-lion Tamarins are now protected and owned by the Brazilian government.

The down side to all this is that animals may be brought into captivity, ostensibly for the purpose of 'breeding to put back into the wild', and unknown stock be introduced to them which in turn invalidates those animals from being part of any proper breeding programme. To introduce these unidentified specimens back into the natural state, would be detrimental to the existing wild stocks.

DANGEROUS WILD ANIMALS

Keeping some of the more dangerous species of animals has been popular in the past, but is not so familiar today because of all the restrictions that help to 'frighten off' people from doing so.

Dwarf crocodile

The Dangerous Wild Animal Act (1976) which came into force to protect such animals, their owners, and the general public, does not make it illegal for anyone to keep any dangerous wild animal, such as a poisonous snake, for example, but what it does say is that there are many rules and regulations that must be applied before a licence is even considered for issue.

These rules and regulations involve many considerations, such as the qualifications of a person to keep such animals, planning issues that may arise especially in sensitive localities such as urban areas, the kind of enclosure and the materials to be used, all health and safety safeguards, including escape procedures, and any other constraints that may be laid down by individual local councils. Under normal circumstances, local councils are usually loath to grant licences to individuals, unless the justification for keeping the animal can be substantiated to be for the animal's well being. Normally, licences are granted to zoos and wildlife parks only if they too can prove that all the necessary rules and regulations can be met.

Once licensed, these organisations are inspected at regular intervals, and new licences issued if the inspectors are satisfied that all the questions on the many pages of the licence application are being complied with. If they are not, then there are set times for them to be rectified, and if after that time they are not resolved to the inspectors' satisfaction, then it is possible that an organisation could be closed down.

THE BENEFITS OF JOINING A CLUB

If you are keen to keep exotic creatures, then there are a variety of clubs and societies to join where you can meet others who keep such animals. These are ideal places to learn more about the creatures you have in mind and, in conjunction with this book, about the various methods of keeping them.

Young Kinkajou

For example, rodent and small mammal clubs can be found in most large towns, and their addresses and telephone numbers can be found at local libraries.

Herpetological groups and societies are involved with the study of reptiles and amphibians as a branch of zoology, and their addresses can also be obtained from local libraries.

Ornithological groups are concerned with the study of birds, and many of their addresses are to be found in the journal *Cage and Aviary Birds*, as well as at local libraries.

In addition there are several monthly magazines such as the *Bird Keeper, Budgerigar World, Cat World, Dog World, Practical Fish Keeping, Fur and Feather, Pony Magazine, Horse and Rider*, the *Reptile* etc., which are also available through newsagents.

There are other magazines which are obtained by subscription, covering many other unusual species of animal, and these contain names and addresses of clubs and organisations that you can join. Main libraries stock some of these magazines, or can give the addresses of the publishers.

Cockatoo

HOW WILD ANIMALS BECAME PETS

The Dog

If we look back into the chronicles of the past, the dog is probably the animal that has been domesticated the longest, and it has yet to be proved which species preceded our modern-day dog, Canis familiaris. The wolf and the jackal are very high on the list, with a possibility of several other wild dogs. It could also have been a combination of several species which were first tamed, and then domesticated throughout the world. What we do know is that the domestic dog has the same number of chromosomes as the wolf, and through DNA testing we should come to a definite solution in the not too distant future.

Timber wolf

In addition, no one has yet ascertained when or where domestication took place, although it would seem that the relationship between man and the dog was purely a case of opportunity. It may have been a simple matter of a dog rummaging around a human settlement for food, to be tamed by one or more of the inhabitants. On the other hand the inhabitant could have been revered as a hunter, and he himself accepted within a pack of hunting dogs as a dominant figurehead.

Whether the dog has continued to benefit from its devotion to man, is a very problematic question, which probably will never be answered. Since the abolition of the dog licensing laws in the UK, a large number of dogs have finished up being mistreated, and many have been let loose on our motorways and in our parks to fend for themselves. Most of these animals have never made it, and have been found lying dead or injured in a ditch or gutter, generally completely starved or having been run over by some unsuspecting motorist.

Pixie

Some people neglect to train their dogs adequately, and find later on that the animals become disobedient and impossible to control, and in many cases this leads to abuse to the animal either physical or mental.

Furthermore, the indiscriminate breeding of dogs has placed an enormous burden on the animal rescue services and sanctuaries across this country alone, endeavouring to find homes for these unfortunate animals.

Neutering of the animal so as not to produce quantities of unwanted puppies is inevitably desirable, if breeding is not required. Sometimes, when so-called 'planned breedings' between mixed species do take place, the resulting offspring can turn out to be substandard specimens, unless a professional breeder is in control. These substandard dogs may be stunted in their growth, or have deformed limbs, making them inferior representatives which nine times out of ten have to be put down.

On the good side, most of the dogs in this country are mongrels, and the majority of these are outstanding animals and much loved pets.

From Pasht to Puss

It is very difficult for scientists and zoologists to pinpoint when cats became part of the human environment. This is initially due to little or no skeletal difference between the older species of domesticated cat, and the wild ones of today. What is known, is that domestication took place in the Near East and Africa.

The word cat is presumed to be a derivation of the Arabic word *qattah*, and equivalent words from the North African dialects. The word puss is believed to have come from the Egyptian divinity named Pasht.

Domestic cat

Cats were domesticated later than other species, probably around 3000 BC, although the verification of this fact is rather controversial. It is said that cats simply arrived and made their presence welcome by getting rid of rodents. In appreciation for this 'service', the Egyptians in particular began worshipping the animals. Later there was a total ban on any slaying of cats, and the Egyptian people began mourning their deaths and mummifying their bodies.

Cats were subsequently introduced into Greece and finally into Italy, in particular Rome. From there they travelled into Northern Europe where their popularity rapidly declined. It is alleged that during the fifteenth century, Pope Innocent VIII began incinerating all cats, as they were believed to be connected with the devil and witches. Some time later, in the nineteenth century, the cat's reputation began to recover once again, and it has now become one of the most appreciated of animals.

Gradually the domesticated cats began to cross-fertilise with wild cats, and this brought about the many different characteristics and colorations we know of today. Now, there is little difference between the domestic and wild varieties, except in the colour, patterns, and length of fur. What we know as the striped tabby cat is nearest to the wild cat, which can still be found in the highlands of Scotland although it is becoming rare in its own right. The American domesticated cat is a descendant of the European variety Felis catus and is called a 'domestic short hair'.

Some other breeds have been given more gracious names, which more often than not are misleading. The Abyssinian does not come from Abyssinia, but is a derivative of a wild European. It is believed that the Persian and Angora long-haired species come from the mountainous areas of the Middle East, and the elegant Siamese is probably a descendant of an Indian breed; cats have been domesticated in India for over 2000 years. The exquisite blue Burmese cats however do come from Burma, though the custom of keeping cats there would have probably originated from foreign traders.

Finally, the tailless Manx cat installed itself on the Isle of Man. Its tail is supposedly a genetic mutation and it creates many problems. Many of the offspring die shortly after birth as the mutation can interfere with the fusing of the spinal column. Nevertheless the cat is surviving, and is still held in high esteem by the islanders.

Original island canary

From Green to Yellow

Canaries have been kept as pets for centuries, and are one of the most popular cage birds. The domestic canary is a descendant of a wild green bird native to the forests of the Canary Islands, off the north-west coast of Africa.

The Spanish vanquished the islanders in the fifteenth century and began a good trade in these little birds, which, it is said, were kept by the islanders as pets. The value of the male bird exceeded that of the female because of its song, and the Spanish exported vast numbers around the globe.

In the late sixteenth century, it is maintained that a ship was wrecked on the shores of an island called Elba, in the Tuscan archipelago. It is further documented that on board was a large breeding cage of these birds, and that they all escaped and became feral (wild or untamed), to the island. Since the canary was already a popular bird, the Italians took advantage of this and bred them incessantly.

Fancy canary

As the eighteenth century advanced, the birds were being bred all over Europe. They are still popular in the Canary Islands, but many of them are now imported into the islands from Europe.

The Cavy (Guinea Pig)

The guinea pig originally came to England on Dutch 'Guineaman' ships, and it is possible this is where its name came from.

Domestic cavy

They originated from Peru, South America, where they were first domesticated and bred for food. They can still be found there, living in their natural mountain habitat.

They are not pigs, although the sounds they make could associate them with the squealing of such animals. They weigh between one and three pounds (450–1350 gms) dependent on the species. As a result of around a thousand years of being domesticated, they are now bred in various shapes, sizes, colours and differing furs.

IN FAVOUR OF DOMESTICATION

So the domestication and breeding of creatures is hardly new. What was exotic yesterday is commonplace today. How much pleasure and benefit we have obtained from the former denizens of Egypt and Peru. It is known that the keeping of animals can help to improve relationships within families, give pleasure to sick people, and improve the lonely lives of old people. It can make us kinder, and better informed about the nature of life on earth. It may even save wildlife from being lost for ever.

Leopard cat

YOU LITTLE HOARDER, YOU!

One morning a young jackdaw was delivered to my front door. A young woman, who had the bird wrapped in a towel, said, "I think it has been blown around by the high winds we have experienced lately, as I found it exhausted in our garden but it still had strength to bite me, hence wrapping it in the towel."

"All I can really do," I replied, "is to give it rest and a good feed and see how it does, then if all is well I shall release it back to the wild." The young woman thanked me and left.

I gave the bird a good feed of mincemeat mixed with a little ground biscuit, which it readily took. Being really hungry, it kept eating until the bowl was completely empty. As the days passed it continued to put on weight and got stronger. Becoming more attached to me was the sign for the bird to be released back to the wild. Taking it to where the lady first found it, I threw it into the air and watched as it circuited the area, then disappeared into the blue yonder. Pleased with the outcome, I drove back home to clean the cage out in readiness for the next occupant.

The following day the jackdaw reappeared. Later it was seen once more but this time it was taking pennies from people's fingers and storing them away. An elderly woman who was watching its antics opened her purse and offered it up to the bird. Immediately it arrived, stood on the woman's hand and peered into the gaping purse. All of a sudden there was a rustle and it flew off into the nearby car park. The woman, now very distraught, came to see me and said that it had taken a ten-pound note. Looking outside, I saw the jackdaw perching up high in a sycamore tree, with the money discarded on the ground. Recovering the note, the woman stormed out of the building. The bird meanwhile had ventured back and carried on taking pennies from the public. I stopped feeding it, to encourage it to find food for itself somewhere else, and within days it had stopped visiting.

2
WILDLIFE AND COUNTRYSIDE ACT 1981

Under Part 1. Section 9 (1) of the above act, it is an offence to take certain animals from the wild (Schedule 5 of the act refers), and some of those animals described in this book: the Common Toad, Common Frog, Adder, Grass Snake, Smooth Snake, Smooth Newt, Palmate Newt, and the Great Crested Newt, are all protected under the act, in as much as the killing, injuring, or taking of any of the above animals is an offence. The Great Crested Newt and the Smooth Snake are classified as endangered species.

Under Part 1. Section 9 (4), it is an offence to damage or destroy, or obstruct access to, any structure or place which any wild animal included in Schedule 5 uses for shelter or protection, or disturb any such animal while it is occupying a structure or place, which it uses for that purpose.

Therefore, when buying or receiving any of the above species, it is advisable to find out where the specimens originated from, in case they contravene the Wildlife and Countryside Act 1981, which could then make you liable to prosecution.

If in doubt, ask. If still in doubt, leave alone.

3
FAMILIAR CREATURES, AND SOME LESS FAMILIAR FACTS

DOGS

As for most animals, there are several concerns to consider when searching for a dog to buy as a pet. The lifespan of the animal varies from breed to breed. Normally the larger the dog the shorter the lifespan, the smaller the dog the longer the lifespan, although there are variations to this rule.

Another consideration is the usefulness of the animal, shall we say as a guard dog. The Doberman and the German Shepherd are well known for their intelligence and ferocity when properly trained, but it is rare to find the two qualities in the same animal. Any dog trained for a specific purpose should be considered a specialist first, and a pet second. Both these breeds can also make superb family pets when the breeding has been correctly achieved. Then again, an exception such as the Golden Retriever and Labrador can be both an efficient hunting dog and a wonderful family pet, especially with children.

Border collie (Jessie)

Not knowing enough about the breed before buying, can easily present the owner with an inappropriate pet. This can be, and invariably is, because of incompatibility, which can be due to the temperament or the demands of the species.

Particularly large varieties need endless daily exercise, amounting to maybe four times a day for at least one hour each session.

Some owners find that they do not have the time within their working day to give much attention to the animal, so therefore it is left on its own for hours on end and this culminates in the animal relieving itself in the home, much to the aggravation of the owner.

Then there is the consideration of what to do if you have to leave an animal in the care of someone else who is not familiar with its special needs.

When thinking of obtaining a dog, it is a good idea even after reading up on the various species and having made an informed decision, to be selective in choosing both the breeder you buy from, and the individual dog that you finally take home.

Never pick the cutest withdrawn runt of the litter because you feel sorry for it. You could have serious problems at a later date. Always go for the largest and the brightest of the bunch, so that you will more likely end up with a healthy, sound animal.

Put your sentiment aside and do not fall for the first wagging tail you come across. Don't forget the 'eyes have it', and almost all puppies are irresistible.

Even when you are 'encouraged' by a kennels to take a full-grown dog because it will possibly be put down if you don't, it is always a difficult decision to make. Most times it is an untrue statement just to get the animal off their hands. If you are out to obtain a puppy so that it can grow up with the family, then be strong and move on to the next pair of inviting eyes.

If the animal is a mongrel and a puppy, then try to find out as much as you can about one or both of its parents, so that you have some idea of what it is going to turn into. The most important factor is the animal's ultimate size, and since beauty is in the eye of the beholder, even the ugliest 'mutt' can be loveable, but may outgrow your home.

When acquiring an adult dog from a kennels or animal shelter, the main consideration is its temperament. Many dogs will seem to be friendly when they encounter affection for the first time from a stranger, since being in the kennels or shelter. What may not be known is the history of ill-treatment or hardship, which led to the animal being institutionalised in the first place. This could make the dog a bad risk for certain families, especially those with young children. Keep sentiment to one side and be prepared to return the animal, if it turns out to be aggressive or unsuitable in any way.

Treat the first two to three weeks as a 'settling-in' period where the dog is concerned. If during this time it shows signs of aggression, refusal to respond to you, or general lethargy, then return it to the 'home' it came from. It is no good having an animal that is unhappy with its new environment, or one that cannot get on with new owners.

Most of the more well known animal organisations not only 'vet' the animal once it has left their charge, but also 'vet' the new owners. Someone should visit your home to check on the conditions the dog is being kept in, and its general welfare. This visit is also to find out if there are any problems which they should be made aware of, and which they may be able to help you with. This is the ideal time to let them know your worries or concerns. Don't leave it to the last minute and finish up with a major crisis on your hands.

CATS

The care and breeding of cats seems to come naturally to those who have looked after them for a long time and cat owners are only too pleased to pass on information. There are numerous books on the subject also.

Most town cats are given free run of the house wherever they are kept, and those in the country and the suburbs are also allowed outdoors as well. Those cats that are accustomed to living indoors are normally free of disease, as they do not come into contact with other animals. However, this does not detract from having them inoculated against feline diseases, as these can be carried on the owner's shoes and clothing and be passed on to the unsuspecting cat at any time.

All cats should be collared (the safety type which stretches), with an appropriate tag or barrel with the owner's name and telephone number enclosed. If a cat is not collared then it could end up as someone else's property, or be picked up as a stray, with its fate at the mercy of the local cattery or maybe some illicit animal organisation.

Cats will eat a variety of foodstuffs, and there are several tinned and dry commercial cat foods to try from. As with many other domesticated animals, it is a case of trial and error to find out what the animal will like. Many people keep food accessible for their cat all day, but this habit should be avoided as it is more beneficial for the animal to have designated times for feeding. This helps to regulate the cat's diet, and also encourages it to show up on a regular basis. It can also be a good way of feeding medication when and if required. If the cat supplements its diet with wild mice and birds, then it is advisable to have it checked out regularly for any intestinal worms.

As a preventive measure, worming should be done on a regular basis, in accordance with the veterinary surgeon's recommendations. Treatment can be carried out by the owner with a proprietary worming tablet obtainable from most pet stores, or directly from a vet.

Giving medication to a cat may not look easy but, after some perseverance and practice, it can be carried out with little distress to the animal.

Most cats vomit from time to time; it is a normal occurrence. They will bring up 'fur balls' after grooming themselves and ingesting the fur, and may also vomit after chewing on grass. Sometimes the vomiting may be because of new food, or simply nervousness. Frequent vomiting with diarrhoea, constipation or refusal of food, should be looked upon as serious and a veterinary surgeon consulted.

A bed for the cat should be its own and not the owner's. Cats carry fleas, and to have these unpleasant creatures hopping onto you for a quick nibble, is not something I would recommend. Most times a cat will sleep anywhere as long as it is warm and comfortable.

Population control is important, and along with that goes the psychological advantages of neutering. Males are less likely to roam, less likely to spray, and less likely to incur fight injuries. Females on the other hand do not go into their noisy and frustrating 'heat' whenever an amorous male is around. Infections of the uterus, and tumours, are reduced, even avoided, later in the cat's life.

Many cat owners have their male cats castrated to eliminate the odour of the urine that is sprayed onto objects, especially within the home. This spraying is part of the animal's make-up to demonstrate its sexual prowess, and territorial rights.

If an owner does not have the intention of breeding from the cat, then it would be advisable to have the female spayed as well.

Cats in good condition, and disease free, can live as long as 15–20 years, giving their owners a long period of affection and loyalty.

Tiddles

CANARIES

Canaries can be purchased from good pet shops, animal dealers and breeders, and there are many varieties to choose from. The two main groups are the 'song canaries' which are bred for their song, and the 'type canaries' which are bred primarily for their appearance, although many of them sing as well.

Although the original canary was green, they are now bred in a rainbow variety of colours, some of which are extraordinarily magnificent. The 'red factor', the 'border fancy', the 'Norwich', the 'Yorkshire', and the 'American singer' are all very popular species.

It is generally best to buy the birds in either the winter or the spring months. The reason for this is that they are particularly delicate and are prone to illness if disturbed during the moulting season. This can last from around July until October.

Females are worth less than males, and 'unsexed' canaries are usually the former. It is difficult to tell the age of a canary unless it has been 'leg rung' more or less at birth, indicating its year of birth and, more often than not, the breeder's initials.

RABBIT, RABBIT, RABBIT

The Romans were known to have kept rabbits and hares, but had difficulty in keeping them contained. The enclosures they built were originally intended for hares and had reasonably low walls, which the animals managed to jump over and escape. When rabbits were housed in the hare enclosures, they managed to tunnel their way out under the walls.

Eventually the Romans realised that both species, which I must add here loathe each other, had to be housed separately and differently.

When the Roman empire declined, the newly established monastic houses succeeded in domesti-cating rabbits, and raised them as a source of food. Since that time the animal has been bred in very large numbers, and many breeds have been

Albino rabbit developed in various colours, shapes, and sizes.

The differing varieties developed as demands changed: animals for meat, those for their fur, some for laboratory use, others for show and exhibition use, and lastly those for 'house-pets'.

Many of the breeds, regardless of their original use, have now become adapted to life with humans. Originally, the most popular variety was the New Zealand White or Albino. Although this breed is still available, the much smaller Dutch species which is bred in a variety of colours, and the tiny Polish which weighs only two to three pounds, around a kilo, have become fond favourites especially among those people with limited space. Other varieties which are available are the giant Flemish, which weighs around twenty pounds (9 kilos), the Lop-eared, which can have ears of over twenty inches long (50cm), and fancy furred varieties such as the Chinchilla, Angora, Silver Fox, Satin and the Rex.

GUINEA PIGS

Among all the varieties to choose from, the most common breeds are the English smooth-coated, the Abyssinian rough-coated, and the long-haired Peruvian. When choosing your pet, ensure that the coat is clean, it has bright, well open eyes, no discharge from the nose or anus, and has no injuries. An ill guinea pig will have semi-closed dull eyes, probably matted fur, wet areas around the anus and be lethargic in its movements. It is best to go to a professional breeder to purchase your animals.

These animals do better if kept in pairs of either sex, or one of each sex if breeding is required, or in groups, but never on their own.

The great advantages of keeping them as pets are that they are odourless, gentle, pleasant to handle, relatively quiet except for an occasional high-pitched whistle, and they are resistant to disease. Unlike some of the other smaller rodents, guinea pigs are not very active or prolific breeders, as in the wild state they have very few predators. It is a documented fact that predation induces breeding.

The gestation period of the sow (female) is reasonably long: at least 70 days, and the litters are small, two to four. They are well developed at birth, in fact miniatures of the parents, eyes open and fully furred. All these attributes contribute to their suitability as household pets.

Incy

FAMILY PETS, AND HOLIDAYS

How many times have you been asked, "Could you look after Tiddles for a week whilst we go away?" or, "We've just got a new pet, or rather Jimmy has, and we were wondering if you could look after it while we go to Spain for a week?"

Tentatively you ask what the animal is.

"Oh it's a tarantula, but it doesn't bite."

Suddenly you remember you have an allergy to spiders so, "No, sorry."

Seriously though, you are only too pleased to be of service, but in your subconscious there is always the question, "What if?"

What if it doesn't eat? What if it doesn't look well? What if it gets out? What if it dies?

In fact these fears are largely unfounded. Yes it will miss the owners initially, but nine times out of ten the average animal or pet soon gets accustomed to the fact that things have changed. As long as it is watered and the food goes into the dish at the right time each day, and it is kept clean and made a fuss of, the animal will carry on with its normal routines. But to try and allay some of those fears which can and probably will present themselves, here are a few handy hints about looking after someone else's pet.

Before owners go away, if they haven't explained fully, then ask how much food is given at each feed and at what times. Watch when Jimmy is feeding the 'whatever' and make notes. It is so easy to say, "Oh yes, that's fine," but when they have gone away and you are there on your own, then you start to doubt yourself. "Did he say two heaped teaspoons or was it two heaped dessert spoons?" or, "Does it have two tablets once a day or one tablet twice a day?" Make physical as well as mental notes.

Does the animal have any treats during the day? Should you give any extra if it comes begging? On most occasions the answer to this will be 'no'. Some animals will take advantage when left in the charge of someone different, even if they do know you.

How often is it handled and should it be handled whilst 'they' are away? Do you feel confident enough to handle it? If not there is always an alternative: leave well alone.

If you are looking after a dog, how many times does it go out each day, and how long is each walk? Make a note of the times. Does it mind wet weather and does it normally wear a waterproof? What is its usual route or routes? Can it be let off the lead? Animals have routines as much as humans. Either consciously or subconsciously we all live by the clock, whether it be an exterior clock such as a watch, or our own inbuilt clocks.

Emma

Is the animal registered with a veterinary surgeon? Make sure you take down the telephone number or at least the name and address. If it doesn't have one, then look one up in the Yellow Pages and make a note of it, just in case.

Does the animal have any peculiarities? For example, on occasions it may limp due to a rheumatic condition. Maybe it starts to shake its back leg due to arthritis which comes on from time to time, especially in the colder months. If Jimmy's tarantula is about to shed its skin, then it will turn on to its back and look dead. What a shock if Jimmy hasn't told you about this happening, and you start preparing a hole in the garden for it to rest in peace, only to find out later that it's still alive! All this information is important, as, if it is not expected, any abnormality with the animal can cause an alarm bell to ring, finishing up with the vet being called for no reason at all, and a hefty bill to follow.

When looking after someone else's pet, whether it be a friend's or one of the family's, routines should be adhered to. Not only should it be fed and watered at the specific times, but also warmth and affection should be administered. A dog or cat which is conditioned to affection on a daily basis may suffer from its withdrawal, no matter how short the time period.

To sum up, carry out 'verbatim' any instructions left by the owner, not forgetting to look out for all those 'peculiarities' which may occur from time to time. Copy any physical gestures, words or commands etc., which the animal has been trained to understand and which may reflect true feelings of love and respect, which will in turn help to relax the animal. Above all give warmth and affection wherever possible, and plenty of TLC (tender loving care) and you won't go far wrong.

COMMUNICATION WITH PETS

As already known, a wagging tail on a cat is an indication that the animal is displeased about something or other, whereas a wagging tail on a dog is completely opposite, and an indication that the animal is friendly or pleased to see you.

When a dog's ears are laid back, then you have nothing to fear. But if a horse has its ears laid back, it could be a dangerous situation. Did you know that if you blow gently into a horse's nostrils and place your arm around its neck, it is an indication of assurance that you are a friend?

Harriet

If you behave in a submissive way to a German Shepherd dog (Alsatian) by showing fear, crouching, or avoiding eye contact, you could awaken its sense of dominance and allow it to get the upper hand with possible unintentional consequences.

Hamster mothers with new offspring may destroy them if the nest is disturbed. This act normally happens in times of great distress, but can be caused simply by someone being curious and wanting to have a look at the babies, just as the mother has assured herself that she and her young are safe.

Snakes and lizards normally show no affection towards humans, but some lizards when rubbed along their spine have been known to close their eyes in utter contentment.

Food is one of the best means of communicating with pets, which attracts their attention and can eventually earn their trust. However it is best policy never fully to trust any animal, no matter how friendly or well trained it may seem.

CRUELTY TO ANIMALS – ANIMAL LEGISLATION

It is illegal in most countries of the world to inflict wilful or wanton pain, suffering, malicious neglect or death upon an animal. This is effective in varying degrees, although in the late 20th century the interest in endangered species of plants and animals gave further strength to many anti-cruelty societies and movements.

Our relatively enlightened attitude has not always been so , and human sympathy with the animal kingdom has varied widely throughout times and cultures. It is documented that Pythagoras the Greek philosopher and mathematician actually taught kindness to animals as a duty. Hundreds of years later, Descartes the French mathematician, philosopher and scientist believed that animals could feel no pain whatsoever, and that none had souls: he called them mere machines.

Through the study of genetics we can now observe how closely mankind and animals are related.

It is inferred that anti-cruelty legislation in the western world came about first in the USA. A law was passed in 1641 in Massachusetts Bay Colony that no man should exercise tyranny or cruelty towards any animal kept for man's use or pleasure. It was not until 1809 that Lord Erskine of Scotland brought forward a bill to prevent cruelty to such animals as the pig, the horse, the ox and the sheep. This bill failed to take effect. In 1822 the Martin Act was passed to stop cruelty to large domestic animals. Then two years later in 1824 Richard Martin, an Irishman from Galway, founded the Society for the Prevention of Cruelty to Animals which was the first society for the welfare of all animals. This society was recognised by Queen Victoria and she subsequently added the prefix 'Royal' to its name. The Royal Society for the Prevention of Cruelty to Animals (RSPCA) was created and is still one of the world's most recognised animal welfare organisations.

France was next to create their Society for the Protection of Animals in 1845. Then came Ireland, Germany, Austria, Belgium and the Netherlands. In the USA, the American Society for the Protection of Cruelty to Animals (ASPCA), was chartered in the state of New York in 1866 through the determination of the anti-cruelty campaigner Henry Bergh.

Nowadays almost every country in the world has some form of animal welfare society or organisation.

TAXONOMY

The classification of living organisms is called taxonomy. Carolus Linnaeus, a Swedish scientist, developed a system of classification which is still used today. This means of identifying animals is an advantage, for being Latin-based it can be used in common throughout all countries. Though it is not necessary for the general reader to know the Latin names of animals, I have included them for general interest, as this knowledge can always be taken further.

The classification list is divided into seven parts: the kingdom, phylum, class, order, family, genus and species.

The kingdom can be either animal or plant. This book is concerned with the animal kingdom.

The phylum tells us evolutionary relationships, e.g. vertebrates (creatures with a backbone), invertebrates (having no backbone).

The class tells us within what group a specific animal falls, e.g. mammals.

The order tells us for example the feeding habits, e.g. carnivores (meat eaters), herbivores (plant eaters).

The family tells us the type of animal e.g. cat, dog, bird, snake.

The genus tells us the group of animals' common characteristics, which may comprise several species, e.g. roaring vocal sound.

The species describes a population of animals which are evolutionarily independent, and carry similar genes for reproduction of the same type, e.g. lion, being a specific animal.

Vertebrates contain five classes of animal: a) PISCES, fish, b) AMPHIBIA, amphibians, c) REPTILIA, reptiles, d) AVES, birds, e) MAMMALIA, mammals.

Fish begin the vertebrate groups, as the earliest fossil record of a vertebrate is a fish, believed to be 500 million years old. These fish were armour plated, very unlike our fish of today, which are scaled and are divided into three classes: a) the jawless fish, e.g. the lamprey, b) cartilaginous fish, e.g. the shark, c) the bony fish, e.g. the herring. Seventy-five per cent of the earth's surface is covered with water, both salt and fresh, and fish continue to adapt to life in water.

Amphibians, which have a dual life, start off in water and move on to land when adult, and go through a metamorphosis from egg to adult. A typical example is the toad, where the aquatic tadpole changes into a land-living adult, until the need for breeding, when it will come back to the water. The young rely on gills to be able to breathe in water, but when adult they rely on their lungs to breathe on land. Some amphibians absorb oxygen through their moist skins into their bodies, a third way of breathing.

Reptiles evolved from amphibians by releasing themselves from an aquatic-linked life, and by developing eggs with shells. Also the skin evolved by becoming scaly, to prevent the animals from losing moisture from the body. They are all cold blooded, and rely on the sun to become active. Some lay eggs, whereas others give birth to live young.

Birds are closely related to the reptiles, as can be seen from the scaling which can be found on their legs and feet, and beaks. Other scales have evolved into feathers. Birds, like mammals, are warm blooded but unlike mammals (with the exception of the Duck-billed platypus and the Spiny anteater) lay hard shelled eggs.

The mammals, we know by fossil evidence, had reptile ancestors. Unlike reptiles, they are warm blooded. They give birth to live young, the young suckle from the mother's mammary glands, they have hair or fur, and all have lungs. Even sea mammals such as the seals, whales, dolphins and porpoises, have lungs, and also have hair or fur covering most or part of their bodies.

Taxonomy therefore shows the relationship between different living organisms and describes them so they can be readily identified.

FOR OUR AMERICAN READERS: CONVERSION TABLES FOR WEIGHTS AND MEASURES

It helps to know that 30cm equals about one foot, and one metre is a little over a yard long.

Degrees Fahrenheit are given throughout the text, since accurate temperature measurements are important for animals' well-being.

Length		
metric		USA
1 millimetre [mm]		0.0394 in
1 centimetre [cm]	10 mm	0.3937 in
1 metre [m]	100 cm	1.0936 yd
1 kilometre [km]	1000 m	0.6214 mile

Area

metric		USA
1 sq cm [cm²]	100 mm²	0.1550 in²
1 sq m [m²]	10,000 cm²	1.1960 yd²
1 hectare [ha]	10,000 m²	2.4711 acres

Mass

metric		USA
1 milligram [mg]		0.0154 grain
1 gram [g]	1,000 mg	0.0353 oz
1 kilogram [kg]	1,000 g	2.2046 lb

Volume/Capacity

metric	USA
1 cu cm [cm³]	0.0610 in³
1 cu metre [m³]	1.3080 yd³
1 litre [l]	1.76 pt

From Metric to US Customary Units

When you know	Multiply by	To find
millimetres	0.04	inches
centimetres	0.39	inches
metres	3.28	feet
	1.09	yards
kilometres	0.62	miles
millilitres	0.20	teaspoons
	0.06	tablespoons
	0.03	fluid ounces
litres	1.06	quarts
	0.26	gallons
	4.23	cups
	2.12	pints
cubic metres	35.32	cubic feet
	1.35	cubic yards
grams	0.035	ounces
kilograms	2.21	pounds
metric ton (1,000 kg)	1.10	short ton
square centimetres	0.16	square inches
square metres	1.20	square yards
square kilometres	0.39	square miles
hectares	2.47	acres

4

RODENTS (Rodentia)

The rodent family is one of the largest in the animal world. There are some 1500-2000 species, so they represent almost half of the mammals. The smallest, which is the Harvest Mouse (Micromys minutus) weighs up to 7g and measures about 25cm in length excluding the tail, while the largest which is the Capybara (Hydrochoerus hydrochaeris), weighs up to 45kg and measures over 1m in length. A capybara spends most of its life in water.

Capybara

Rodents are herbivorous, scavenging animals. Their incisor teeth are reduced to one pair in each jaw, with enamel on one surface only, but these grow continually. By the animals' incessant gnawing, they are simultaneously sharpened and kept at a constant length.

Some rodents have folds of skin which can be used as cheek pouches, where food can be stored until required, and many can handle this food with their forelimbs.

Many owners of exotic species also keep rodents for one reason or another, e.g. food for their animals. These rodents also need to be cared for properly, especially to avoid transference of disease.

RATS (Rattus rattus) AND MICE (Mus musculus)

Rats and mice have been favourites with children for many years, due to the fact they are friendly, cheap to feed, and require hardly any management. Although many people

Harvest mouse

House mouse

may think they are all pests and create smells, all mice and rat owners beg to differ. The fancy mouse has evolved from the common House Mouse, and is available in a variety of colours, priced from £1 ($1.45) each. If looked after properly, they create no unpleasant smells.

The same goes for the rat, which has evolved from the Common Brown rat, and more and more people are realising that these creatures are really very clean and make interesting pets, and like the mouse are reasonably priced from £3 ($4.50) each.

With rats and mice, the females are called does and the males bucks.

When selecting your rat or mouse, look for a healthy one, which should have shiny fur and eyes that are bright and bold. An unhealthy specimen will have a dull and uneven coat, rough to the touch. The eyes may appear sunken and the animal listless. In addition look for any body sores, bald patches, lumps and kinks in the tail. These animals have either been mismanaged or have some dietary deficiency. Good quarters, a balanced diet, and fresh water at all times, are essential for a healthy animal.

As with all rodents, a suitable plastic or metal cage is preferable, due to the fact it can be washed out properly and dried so as to prevent any infection arising. Clean the cage once a week, except when new-born are in the nest, and add a little disinfectant to the cleaning water. Any urine-wetted floor material should be taken out daily. Sawdust and wood shavings are ideal litter for the base of the cage, plus a ball of hay.

The cage size can vary, depending on the species of the animal kept, although the larger the cage the better. A suggested minimum size for a pair of mice is 60cm long by 23cm deep by 23cm high, and for a pair of rats 1m long by 30cm deep by 30cm high.

A suitable nesting area should be readily available for the mouse, such as a wooden box with a 3.75cm hole drilled in it to allow easy access. Rats will normally nest out in the cage on hay. Plenty of toys such as cotton

Brown rat

reels, a ladder, tree branches and rocks, should be available for your pet mouse or rat, but be very careful with the 'treadmill wheel', as the centre spindle does tend to rub the back of the animal, creating sores.

Feeding your pet mouse or rat is simple. A variety of seeds, flaked maize, bran, stale but not mouldy brown bread, with a little cabbage, carrot, apple, pear, tomato and nuts would constitute a balanced diet. Give fresh water at all times, preferably in a water bottle, which prevents contamination of the water. Bowls get tipped over, thereby wetting bedding.

Mice, because of their light weight, can be picked up by the base of the tail. Rats need more care when handled. Put one hand over the back of the rat and lift it up on to the other hand for support. After a time your pet rat will probably walk on to the hand, but you will still need to steady him with the other hand.

A female mouse can produce her first litter at 6 weeks of age, and then again at 6-week intervals. The litters can range from one cub up to 14 at a time. It is possible for one female to give birth to over 100 cubs per year This is, naturally, an extreme example.

It is better to separate the male from the female when signs of pregnancy occur, to enable her to have her babies in peace and quiet.

Gestation is 19 to 21 days, and extra hay should be given within this time, for the nest. When born, the cubs are pink, blind, toothless and furless. Within 8 days the eyes are open, by 12 days they have their teeth, although they will suckle up to 30 days.

The breeding of rats is a little different. The male can be left in the cage with the female at pregnancy. The gestation period is 21 to 23 days, with an average of 7 cubs per litter. Weaning of rats is quicker than mice, around two to three weeks. They start to breed at 12 to 16 weeks.

RABBITS (Oryctolagus cuniculus)

Although rabbits look and act like rodents, they are taxonomically called LAGOMORPHS (they are believed to have diverged from a primitive stock soon after the rodents). Lagomorphs have an extra, peg-like incisor tooth on either side of the normal incisors, and the molars and pre-molars are also set differently and used for cutting. Therefore the upper teeth bite outside the lower ones. Unlike rodents, lagomorphs can open and close their nostril flaps, and have short tails. Within the order are rabbits, hares and cottontails.

Sexing of rabbits can be difficult for the untrained, but the easiest method is with the male, as the penis can be extruded by applying pressure either side of the genital orifice. The male is called the buck and the female the doe. Rabbits cost from £3 ($4.50) each depending on the variety.

A healthy rabbit is very alert, self-grooms, and is continually searching its habitat. An ill rabbit shows signs of diarrhoea, noisy breathing, continual rubbing of the snout, ruffled coat and huddling up. To prevent illness, good quarters, a balanced diet and fresh water are essential, and good management of the animal.

The ideal quarters are either plastic or metal, so they can be dismantled and cleaned twice a week, and disinfected once a week, but a large purpose-built wooden hutch will suffice. Cleanliness is especially important for rabbits. Suitable types of litter for the base of the cage are sawdust, wood shavings and straw. For the nest sites use hay.

A doe requires a nest box during the last week of her pregnancy, and throughout the period of weaning and rearing her young. A cardboard box is ideal.

Just before the young are born, she will start to pull out fur from under her throat and begin to line her nest with it. This is a quite normal.

When breeding, always take the doe to the buck for copulation, never the other way round, else the doe will attack the buck. This can be repeated two or three hours later to ensure mating has taken place.

Gestation is about 30–32 days, and the doe can produce up to 10 young at a time.

Young rabbits are ready for breeding when only 6 to 9 months old, depending on the species.

Feeding can get complicated if you allow it, but it is advisable to give a pelleted diet, supplemented with green stuffs such as lettuce and cabbage, carrot and a little apple. Tomatoes can be given in moderation, as they contain high levels of vitamin C. Water is best given in a proprietary rabbit bottle which has a screw-on drip pipe, which the rabbit can lick when it wishes. This ensures that fresh water is available at all times.

When handling rabbits, always lift them by the scruff of the neck, never by the ears, and support their hind quarters with your other hand.

SIBERIAN CHIPMUNK (Eutamias sibericus)

These are small burrowing rodents, full of activity and curiosity. They are also excellent climbers and in the wild state live in forests. They can be caged singly, in pairs or in groups of one male to two females.

Whether you keep them indoors or outdoors, large cages are essential. A minimum of 1.2m long by 1m deep by 2m high, would suffice one pair comfortably, and should have one, or at best two, solid sides. The base of the cage should

Siberian chipmunk

be secure so as to help baffle escapes. It should be made of concrete, marine ply or wire, and covered deeply with straw, peat, wood shavings or sawdust. A good scattering of leaves should then cover the base. Shelves, branches, rocks, pipes, and nest boxes will provide interest and exercise.

For outdoor enclosures, some form of shelter against inclement weather should be included in the design. As these are very active and very fast-moving animals, it is also important to have a double door on the cage, to prevent escape. Wire mesh size should be 25mm by 12.5mm by 16g, since anything larger will allow the animals to get out, and chicken wire is hopeless as it can be bitten through.

Nest-boxes are required, one per adult, 150mm deep by 200mm high by 150mm wide minimum, with an entrance hole of about 50mm diameter half way up one side, and a good amount of bedding material consisting of dry leaves or hay, which should fill the box. Site the boxes just above ground level, and put extra bedding in the cage in autumn, for a female with young.

Inside cages should be cleaned every fortnight with a mild solution of water and detergent, or bacteria and smell will build up, and faecal droppings should be taken out regularly. One corner of the cage is usually used as a lavatory, so this makes the task simple. Avoid using disinfectants of any type. The cleaning of outside cages is not necessary as the natural elements will cope with this, although it is still advisable to pick up faecal droppings, or wasted fruit, on a daily basis. Nest boxes should be taken out and thoroughly washed and dried once or twice a year, especially after a litter of young have been weaned. Don't touch the nest boxes between the months of September and March, because there will be seeds hoarded inside them.

Heating the cages is unnecessary since these animals are of a temperate breed, but they do need good ventilation.

Chipmunks are really vegetarian and need a good balanced diet of nuts, seeds, fruit and vegetables. A commercial hamster mix can be used with added sunflower seeds and nuts. Give a little fruit each day, selecting from apple, pear, tomato, grapes and seasonal fruits. Stones from many fruits can be poisonous to some chipmunks, so remove these before feeding. Dandelion leaves, whole peas, corn cobs, cucumber, lettuce etc. can also be given, in small amounts until you find what your animal really likes. A commercial mixed nut assortment is ideal and gives variety. Also, include wild acorns and sweet horse chestnuts. Fortunately chipmunks cannot be overfed, as any food not eaten will be stored by them, either dug into the ground or hoarded in the nest box.

When putting branches into the cage, try when possible to get apple or oak. The constantly growing incisor teeth need hard materials to gnaw on to prevent them from getting too long. Also, pectin in the apple wood is beneficial to the animals' diet.

Some chipmunks like insects from time to time, so giving mealworms and crickets, in moderation, is beneficial to them. Breeding females should be offered milk-based foods such as baby cereal, mixed with warm water and honey to a soup-like consistency.

Chipmunks start breeding at around one year old. The continual chirruping of the female indicates that mating has probably been successful. Once this has happened, separate the male from the female, so she can have peace and quiet.

Gestation lasts for around 31 days. After birth, the female tends to stay in the nest box most of the time, and should not be disturbed. The young emerge from the nest at just over a month old and, if necessary, can be separated from the mother about 10 days later.

Although some females have another litter during late summer, it is normal for them to only have one per year.

Aggression is common in chipmunks, mainly during the autumn, when collection of winter food stores is taking place. If one animal has been kept on its own, never put another into its cage, because they will definitely fight. It is always better to put both animals into a new cage together, when they are young. The only time this rule is broken, is when putting a breeding male to a female on heat.

Animals kept outdoors will probably hibernate during the winter months, so it is important to make sure the entrances of the nest boxes are sheltered from the rain, and that the boxes are well insulated. They also will hibernate in the ground if there is 60cm or more depth of soil or other substrate. They may not be seen from October through to March, which can be worrying for some people, but it's best to leave them and not start digging around to see if they are all right. They will soon emerge once the weather starts to warm.

Those animals caged indoors will probably become sluggish, and remain in the nest box for a few days at a time, during the winter months.

Chipmunks do not like a lot of noise, and loud sounds may create hyper-activity due to stress. They are also sensitive to the radiation from television sets, and any prolonged exposure could result in death.

Chipmunks do not like to be handled, so, if you have to move one, do it at night when it is in the nest box. Cover the entrance hole, and the box can then be used as a carry box, and the amount of stress caused to the animal will be minimal. Other than this, a light-weight net can be used, but any continual chasing to catch the animal can result in severe stress, and should be avoided at all costs. The first method is much the best.

Always keep an eye on the incisor teeth, as with all rodents, and if there is any sign of them becoming too long, due to too much soft food or another cause, then macaroni can be given for the animal to gnaw. If this fails, then the teeth may need cutting, so consult your veterinary surgeon for advice. As with all animals, if a chipmunk becomes ill, loses its appetite, or remains inactive with its fur fluffed up, go to the section on first aid (p.127), and at the same time call your veterinary surgeon. Chipmunks can live very happily in captivity, for up to 10 years, provided all the health and management rules are carried out as outlined in this chapter.

Silver chinchilla

CHINCHILLA (Chinchilla laniger)

This animal, like the guinea pig, once inhabited the mountains of Peru, Bolivia, northern Chile and western Argentina, and is now almost exclusively a domesticated animal, which is raised in captivity for its silver fur. The Chinchilla has become rare in the wild because of hunting, and most of the 'elegant' coats made from chinchilla skins once came from the wild animal, but nowadays come from animals in captivity. These coats take around 200 skins each to make.

Chinchillas are available in some of the larger pet shops, and although they are not as bright as a rat or as submissive as a guinea pig, they are active, alert, and friendly creatures.

As with some other rodents, quick movements that may startle or surprise the animal can lead to them biting in self defence, but with careful handling they can become very tame and enjoyable. I say *careful* handling because the coat of this animal is not as dense as other rodents, and the silky fur does tend to come away very easily, especially with the moisture on the hands. When picking one up, carefully lift it by the base of its tail, and then support the animal with the other hand. Try to 'cuddle' it in your arms and not your hands, and this will avoid fur loss.

They can tolerate a wide range of temperatures, 5°C–25°C (40°–75°F), and like rabbits can live outdoors in the summer months, but they must have suitable protection from rain and draughts.

Caging can be the same as for the rabbit, although these animals do like to climb. A tall cage, 2m high, 1m deep and 1m wide, with branches at different levels, will make a suitable home for your chinchilla. A small sleeping box can be adjoined to the main cage, so the animal has privacy when it wishes and a separate area to sleep. In addition to this, a shallow pan of 'silver sand' or 'Thames sand' should be placed in the cage every day, so that it can 'dust bath', which helps to keep the silky coat clean. Droppings and uneaten food should be taken out of the cage daily, and the cage cleaned thoroughly once a week.

A pellet has been devised for chinchillas in captivity, which is a good base to the diet. Try offering small quantities of lettuce and carrot, and possibly apple, in addition to the pelleted food, along with fresh hay. It is essential that fresh water is available, if your animals are fed on dry foods, which nowadays is normal as they contain all the nutrients, minerals and vitamins required. In the wild they eat a form of lichen, which is found high up in the Andes mountains, and take their water from the dew on the rocks early in the morning.

Chinchillas are reasonably easy to breed in captivity, but it is best to keep them in separate cages, as they have a tendency to be aggressive to each other.

They are ready for mating from about 6 months. Gestation is long, around 111 days, but the youngsters, which average two to a litter, are born with eyes open and are well developed at birth. They are weaned at about 2 months old. The males can remain with the females during this period, although it is common practice to remove the male for a day or so when the babies are born.

Chinchillas as pets may live to around 5 or 6 years of age, although some have lived much longer.

FOR GOODNESS SAKE FLY AWAY!

A woman rang me one day. "I have this bird which I have raised on scraps," she informed me, "but now it is getting too large for me to handle so would you like it?"

"What kind of bird is it?" I asked. "I do not have the room for ordinary wild birds, but I can put you in touch with someone who does."

"It is brown in colour and has very sharp claws," said the woman, "so could you come and have a look at it and let me know?" I got into my car and set off on another of my little adventures. On arriving at the place, I was led into a small shed and there sitting on the ground was a fully developed buzzard. Somewhere along the line it had broken the tip of its beak and it was having difficulty in tearing its own food. The woman told me that she had always hand-fed the bird because she realised it was not eating properly. I explained to her what it was and that I would take it back with me, but it would eventually be released to the wild once the beak had sufficiently regrown and it could fend for itself.

On arrival at the zoo the buzzard was fed on slivers of meat and it quickly filled its crop. It was obvious that it was starving. Over the following weeks the beak grew to such a length that the bird was now capable of tearing its own food, and I was ready to give it its first chance to go back to the wild. Taking it to near the place it was found, I threw it into the air, and after three attempts it flapped and soared and disappeared out of view. Feeling happy at the thought the bird had survived, I ventured back home.

On my arrival, I noticed a large bird sitting on the fence. The buzzard had come back! All it could do was to scream for food, so feeling sorry for it I gave it a feed. I tried again to release it, this time a little further away. Again it was there waiting for me when I arrived back.

I knew of a sanctuary which kept all manner of birds, so I contacted them and asked if they had room for a buzzard.

"We could put it in an aviary with other buzzards and see how it settles, but eventually it will be released back to the wild," said Pete the sanctuary owner. The bird was taken to the sanctuary and it settled in well, but after six months with no human contact it was released into the wild many times, only to come back to the sanctuary each time, and it remained there until its natural demise.

5

THE WORLD OF BIRDS

RELATIONSHIP OF HUMANS TO BIRDS

The fascination of caging wild birds goes back to ancient times, possibly further back than the Egyptians. Many species of indigenous 'victims' have been caught and transferred to small cages, either for their song, their colour, or for the table. The humble chicken, bred in profusion in most countries, is probably the most devoured of the game birds. The turkey is possibly a close second along with the pheasant, the grouse, and the quail.

Domestic pigeon

Although the caging of birds still happens, the methods used are far more humane than in the past. In many countries, for example the USA and the UK, minimum requirements of cage and aviary sizes are laid down, and must be adhered to for the welfare of the animals. Any disregard of these statute requirements could be conceived as an act of cruelty to them, leading to heavy fines or even imprisonment. It would also induce the confiscation of the animals in question.

In the UK it is illegal to take birds from the wild, unless a licence is issued by the Secretary of State, under the Wildlife and Countryside Act (1981). Many birds bred nowadays have come from original 'wild stocks'. These offspring are seen for sale in pet shops, and also in the many bird trade newspapers and magazines.

When looking at the various birds for sale within the different countries of the world, we find that in general terms they are the same varieties. Below I have listed a few of the many cage and aviary birds that are available here in the UK and also in the USA.

CAGE AND AVIARY BIRDS

Tanagers   Small brightly coloured birds; the males are glossy black above and either orange or yellow on their under parts. They have short, stout beaks and short tails. They live in the forests of Central and South America as well as the West Indies. Their diet consists of various insects including beetles, moths, bees, and wasps, and fruit, especially mistletoe berries. The enveloped nests are built in trees and have a side entrance. They lay 2-5 eggs and incubate for 11–14 days.

Manakins   This is a family of small, dumpy, short-tailed birds which have short, broad, slightly hooked beaks. They also have short wings. They are basically black with coloured heads and caps. They inhabit the tropical forests of Central and Southern America and nest in bushes and trees. They lay 1–3 eggs and incubate 19–28 days. Their diet consists of various fruits and insects.

Weavers   Again these are small, stocky birds with short, stout beaks. They are mainly black and yellow birds and many have black heads and faces. They are very sociable birds which inhabit the woodlands and grasslands of Africa and South Asia. They build woven nests which are suspended from trees. These nests can take on a variety of shapes and sizes and are colonial in their usage. Weavers lay 2–4 eggs and incubate 11–17 days. They feed on a variety of seeds and insects.

Waxbills   This is a very varied family of small, brightly coloured finches, although some are dull but with striking markings. They have rounded wings and medium to short tails. Their bills are short and conical in shape, and vary between large and small. They are very gregarious and primarily inhabit the forests, grasslands and deserts in Africa. Some species can also be found in Australasia, South Asia and the Pacific Ocean Islands. They build a domed nest which, like the tanagers', has a side entrance; some species nest in holes. They lay 4–8 eggs and incubate 10–21 days. They feed primarily on small seeds such as millet, and insects.

Bullfinches   These birds come in a variety of colours, such as grey, red, orange and brown. They have black tails and wings with white rumps. Most have a black face or black cap and short stout beaks. They inhabit woodlands in Europe, Asia and the Azores. They nest in trees and feed off berries, seeds and buds of fruit trees, making them an unwelcome pest in fruit growing areas. They lay 3–5 eggs and incubate 12–14 days.

Leafbirds   Bright green coloured birds with pointed, curved beaks. They live in the woods and forests of South and South East Asia, Indonesia, and the Philippines. They feed on fruit, especially figs, berries, and nectar from flowers. They build cup-shaped nests in the trees. Lay 2–3 eggs and incubate about 14 days.

Mynahs   These reasonably large birds are mainly black or dark brown. They have white at the base of the primary feathers and white on the tip of the tail. Being omnivorous they eat a variety of foodstuffs that includes insects, fruits and berries. They nest in holes in trees or in banks of earth, and come from South Russia and China, into South East Asia, then across to Celebes. They lay 2–7 eggs and incubate 11–18 days. They have been introduced into Australasia and South Africa. Two main species are the Hill Mynah and the Bank Mynah. Both are good mimics.

Mynah

Toucans   This medium-sized family of birds has a black throat and
             back with a green metallic burnish. The rump is very bright
             red with a long tail. The underneath of the bird is yellow
             with bands of red and black across the breast. The beak is
             basically ivory in colour, with black and red markings, and
             the wings are short and rounded. They inhabit forest regions
             of Central and South America and nest in tree hollows. They
             lay 2–8 eggs and incubate 12–14 days. They feed generally
             on fruit, but have been known to take small rodents and
             insects.

Cardinals   This family ranges from small to medium finches with heavy
             bodies and large conical beaks. The males are often highly
             coloured. They live in the woodlands of North, Central, and
             South America and nest in trees. They lay 2–5 eggs and
             incubate 11–14 days. They feed off fruits, insects, flower
             blossom and seeds.

Orioles   These are mainly black and yellow, black and red, or green
             birds. They have very stout black, red or blue beaks and feed
             on insects and fruits and nest in trees. They lay 2–4 eggs and
             incubate 14–15 days. Some have red bare skin around the
             eyes. They are found in Europe, Africa, Asia and Australasia.

Quetzals   Medium to large birds with bright green or brown backs.
             Their heads are green, blue or violet, as are their throats. The
             breasts of the birds vary in colour from pink, red, orange and
             yellow. They have rounded wings and long squared-off tails
             in the females. They inhabit the forests and clearings of
             Central and South America. They feed off insects and fruits,
             and nest in holes in trees and termite nests. They lay 1–8
             eggs and incubate 11–14 days.

Cotingas   This family of birds range from small to large. They are
             brightly coloured and some have facial wattles, and crests.
             They normally nest in trees and bushes and are found in

Central and South America. The nest is open-cup shape although the species 'Cock-of-the-rock' builds a mud and vegetable nest, usually on a rock face. They lay 1–3 eggs and incubate 19–28 days. They feed off insects and fruits, taking the insects whilst in flight.

Antbirds   A family of small to medium sized birds coloured grey, black or brown. This coloration is sometimes streaked or barred. They have short to long tails and short, rounded wings. The beak is strong and can either be slightly or very hooked. They inhabit forest and scrubland within Central and South America. They build hanging nests from branches or in tree holes, or build on the ground, depending on the species. They lay 2 eggs and incubate 14–16 days. They are insectivorous and are identified by their devouring of ants.

Flycatchers   Small to medium birds with dull olive plumage above and yellow or white underneath. Some species have various other colours such as chestnut and white, red, orange; some have crown stripes and many have crests. The beak is broad with a hooked tip. The wings are short and rounded on some species but long and pointed on others. The tail is average but square. They feed off insects and fruit although some have been known to take mice, frogs and other birds. They weave cup-shaped nests in the trees, globular ones with side entrances, and hanging nests. Some also make nests on the ground. They lay 2–8 eggs and incubate 14–20 days. Found in the forests and open country of North, Central and South America.

PARROTS (Psittacines)

The parrot family is well known to most people. Budgerigars (Melopsittacus undulatus) and Cockatiels (Nymphicus hollandicus) are the two most popular ones to be kept as pets. These two species originate from Australia, but are now bred in large numbers in this country.

African Grey

Both the African Grey parrot (Psittacus erithacus), a much larger bird, and the Amazona parrot from South America have also been domesticated. Parrots normally have blunt, short tails, but the parakeets and lorikeets are distinguished by their longer tails, as are the macaws.

Nearly all parrots are monomorphic in colour, which means that both sexes are the same. The exception is the Eclectus parrot (Eclectus roratus) where the male is basically green and the female red.

Listed below are the different families of parrots, with their distinctive peculiarities.

Cockatoos (Cacatua)

Sulphur Crested cockatoo

These birds come from Australia, some of the South Pacific islands, and the Philippines, and most are good talkers.

They are very active birds, and live longer than most parrots. The Greater Sulphur Crested Cockatoo (Cacatua galarita) has been known to surpass one hundred years of age.

In general, cockatoos are hardy birds and can stand most climates. They thrive in captivity, but need attention all the time, especially if a single bird is owned. When they suffer from lack of attention, pining for a mate, or poor diet, feather plucking is common with captive species. Their feathers are covered in a very fine powder, which gives the appearance of chalk, and can be an irritant to people with chest problems.

The largest of the cockatoos is the Palm Cockatoo (Probosciger aterrimus), which comes from New Guinea, and measures 75cm in length. A good diet should consist mainly of seeds, nuts and fruit.

Macaws (Ara)

These birds are to be found from Mexico to Paraguay and Southern Brazil, and are much more colourful than cockatoos. The Hyacinth (Anodorhynchus hyacinthinus) is the largest, measuring 86cm in length.

Macaws are the only parrots with facial patches, which distinguish them from other parrots, such as the Conure.

The Blue and Gold macaw (Ara ararauna) and the Green Winged (Ara chloroptera) are the two most common birds to see or buy; whereas the Scarlet macaw (Ara macao) is now becoming very rare in the wild.

Their diet consists of seeds, nuts and fruit.

Green Winged macaw

Conures (Aratinga)

These come from Mexico, southwards through most of South America.

They have a long slender shape, with a long tapering tail, large head and large beak. They also have a bare ring around the eyes. They are like macaws, but in miniature.

Most species are readily available from pet shops, and they feed mostly on seeds, nuts and fruit.

Parakeets (Psittacula)

These come from India, China, Sri Lanka and Africa. All have a ring of colour that starts at the throat and flares outwards and downwards around the neck. Their body colour is green, with other pastel colours.

The most common species to be found for sale are the Indian Ringneck (Psittacula krameri borealis), African Ringneck (Psittacula krameri krameri), and the Plum Head (Psittacula cyanocephala). The Budgerigar (Melopsittacus undulatus) is the most common; it is a grass parakeet from Australia.

Diet is mainly small seeds, and a little fruit.

Lovebirds (Agapornis)

These originate from Africa, and are really miniature parrots. They range between 10 and 15cm in length, and are brightly coloured. Unlike some other parrots, they lay 3 or 4 eggs per nest.

Diet consists of seeds, grits, cuttlefish bone, green foods etc.

Lories and Lorikeets (Loriidae)

These range in habitat from New Guinea, the Molucca Islands, the

Philippines, Bali and the surrounding islands. They are hardy birds that take readily to captivity, and are easy to breed once established.

In their natural habitat they are nectar-drinking birds, using a brush-like tongue to collect nectar from flowers. Several diets have been tried to simulate the nectar that they require, starting with honey water, but this did not contain sufficient vitamin content, so evaporated milk was added to the mixture. This tended to create problems with a build-up of food collecting in the lower mandible, which in turn created a mould similar to thrush in humans, called candida albicans. This mould eventually got into the respiratory tract, and more or less suffocated the bird. Antibiotics are available to treat moulds, and these should be administered as soon as the mould is first seen. Better still, do not give the mould-inducing form of diet.

Black-capped lory

Nowadays, the diet in captivity consists of a proprietary fruit-flavoured baby cereal, mixed with warm water to a milky consistency. Some lories will eat a little fruit and sunflower seeds, as well as the nectar mix. There are also other proprietary 'nectar diets' available on the open market.

Lories and lorikeets, like other birds, bathe regularly. In captivity they can easily soil their feathers, due to the liquid feed. Therefore it is necessary to put clean water into the cage for bathing, as well as drinking water.

Pygmy Parrots (Micropsitta)

These come from New Guinea, the Solomon Islands and surrounding islands.

Not normally seen in captivity, due to their uncertain feeding habits, it is presumed that they feed mainly on fungi, and termites, and the grubs of other insects living in rotting wood.

Other Parrots

There are three other species of parrots, and these are declining in numbers very rapidly.

- ### Kakapo (Owl Parrot) (Strigops habroptilus)

   This comes from New Zealand and is a nocturnal species which is disappearing in the wild. It eats roots, seeds, fruit and grasses.

- ## Kaka (Brown Parrot) (Nestor meridionalis)
These also come from New Zealand and are vanishing rapidly. They live on insects, insect larvae and nectar from flowers.

- ## Kea Parrot (Nestor notabilis)
This is another species from New Zealand which is becoming rarer in the wild; nonetheless it is considered a pest as it is very destructive to farm crops. It can be seen in zoos, although breeding has been very limited. It feeds mainly on carrion and insects, but fruit and roots are also a major part of its diet.

Kea

GET YOUR SNOUT OUT OF MY NOSE!

I once went to some television studios with one of my birds, Charlotte the Scarlet Macaw. A friend called Steve, from another zoo, was there with a Coati, an animal similar to a Raccoon. It was arranged by the studio that the two animals with the keepers were to be on the set of *Children in Need* at the same time. This did not bother me, as both animals were getting on well together, and they would not come into direct contact with each other. Taking Charlotte onto the set, I was met by the presenter, who was a local naturalist and photographer. The Coati entered with Steve and all sat down in readiness.

Just as the cameras began to roll the Coati put its snout up Steve's nose, making it bleed quite badly. With quick presence of mind, Steve pushed some tissue up his nose to stop the bleeding and the interview went ahead. Charlotte meanwhile had sensed something was amiss and proceeded to laugh. It was such a raucous laugh that Steve could not be heard when the interviewer questioned him, the audience became infected by the bird's laugh, and the whole studio was in turmoil. Pledges were made to meet Charlotte and the offending Coati at their appropriate zoos, and well over £900 was raised for the charity. The studio bosses were still laughing as we left the set.

SERIEMA (Cariama cristata)

There are only two species of seriema and both are long-legged birds with long necks and elongated bodies. They live on the grasslands and open

scrub of South America. Their range is Brazil, Eastern Bolivia, Uruguay, Paraguay, and Northern Argentina. It is documented that these birds may be descendants of an extinct ground-dwelling bird that was purely carnivorous. This knowledge has been gleaned from fossils found within the South Americas.

The Red-legged or Crested seriema, although not a ratite (flightless bird), very rarely flies but can run very fast to escape danger. Its diet is primarily reptiles and amphibians, but it will

Crested/Red-legged
Seriema chick

also feed off insects, leaves and seeds. Its broad, sharp, pointed beak is a good weapon to impale any unfortunate animal that may come its way.

Its nests are built within low trees or bushes from sticks, and two or three eggs are laid. Incubation is around 26 days, and in that time both parents help to incubate the eggs. The chicks will remain in the nest until they are well grown, almost adult.

In South America they are hunted for their meat so they have become very shy birds, wary of humans. They are also sometimes taken from their nest by farmers and raised with their ground fowl. If any predators approach the farm then the seriemas begin screaming and yelping, so they are very useful as watchdogs, similar to geese.

OWLS

The owl family are small-to-large silent fliers of the night, although some species can be seen during the day. They have large heads, with large round forward-facing eyes, short necks, powerful claws and short, strong, hooked beaks. In addition they have facial discs which help to pick up and concentrate sound, and many have ear tufts. They feed on small rodents and other small mammals, birds, fish, and insects. They can be found inhabiting forests, grasslands,

Eagle owl   deserts, open country including the frozen wastes of the

Arctic, (Snowy Owl). Depending on the species they nest in holes in trees or in burrows. There are some 22 genera (group of animals with the same structural characteristics), and over 120 species, some of which do migrate, and can be found all over the world. They, like all other wild birds, are protected, and it is illegal to take them or their eggs from the wild, (Wildlife and Countryside Act 1981). Here I have listed three species that can be obtained through licensed breeders, or through larger pet stores.

Barn Owl (Tyto alba)
One of the most widespread birds, found on all continents except for Antarctica, it also has the name of 'screech owl' which has arisen from its eerie call. It is some 35cm in length and has a wing span of up to 90cm. They are normally a resident bird but have been known to travel some 1000 kilometres (625 miles). They are purely nocturnal birds, having a series of different calls from a hissing sound to a blood-curdling screech.

Their diet is mainly mice and rats and on occasions frogs, lizards and some other small birds, which are swallowed whole. As with all owls the indigestible parts of the prey, such as the fur and the bones, are regurgitated in the form of a large pellet. On average a single barn owl will eat some 100 g, around four mice, of food daily. They can live up to 20 years or more, and are sexually mature between the age of one and two. They nest in old ruins, barns, dead hollow trees and cliff cavities, and can lay up to 7 glossy, white eggs which take 30–32 days to hatch. The eggs are normally laid one every two or three days which means that the young hatch at the same intervals. Once all young are hatched there is a considerable difference in size between the first born and the last. This can create problems, as the first born has been known to eat the last born. The offspring are fledged 65 days after hatching and are fully independent of the parents after a further month.

Because of the clearing of rough ground which is taking place today, and the disappearance of barns, their favourite nesting place, the barn owl is gradually dwindling in numbers. The ideal terrain for these birds is farmland with hedges, small forests, ditches and wooded clearings.

Tawny Owl (Strix aluco)

The largest of the British owls, around 37cm long, it has a very big head and a stout body, with small hooked beak and powerful claws. The bird is resident in most parts of Britain but is not found on the Isle of Man, some of the Scottish islands or in Ireland. It can be seen within the city boundaries but its main habitat is the wooded countryside. Unlike the barn owl's screeching sound this owl has the unmistakable 'too-wit too-woo' call. They are active by night but can be seen flying during the day, especially when they have been disturbed. Whilst walking through a forest or copse, you may see them in the upper branches pushed up against the trunk of a tree. It has often been documented that these birds enjoy the sun and have been seen to sunbathe.

They hunt by night by means of their acute hearing, and feed mainly off rodents such as mice and rats and will also take frogs, fish, insects, roosting birds and various other small mammals.

They nest in the holes of trees, in rocks and buildings and sometimes even on the ground. Two to four white eggs are laid and these take some 28 days to incubate. As with the barn owl the eggs are laid at intervals, so the resulting fledglings hatch large down to small. Again this can present problems with the larger youngsters eating the smaller, but this is not such a common event. The young are fully fledged after a further 35 days but will on occasions leave the nest before this time. Because of deforestation many tawny owls are disappearing, but they are less scarce than barn owls.

Eurasian Eagle Owl (Bubo bubo)

The largest European owl, it has been known to reach 90cm long, although the average is 75cm, the females being the larger of the two sexes. Although sometimes called the European eagle owl, its range spreads from Europe into North Africa and Asia. It has a reasonably large head, small hooked beak, very large powerful pointed talons, large ear tufts and very large orange eyes: the distinctive features of this owl.

They have been known to inhabit parts of Britain in the past, and it has been documented that a pair lived on a hillside in south-west Scotland in the spring of 1941, and behaved as if they were nesting. Since that time there have been some unsubstantiated sightings, especially in Scotland. They are believed to have taken rabbits, various birds, rats, mice and water voles for food, although in other parts of Europe they have been known to take larger animals up to the size of a roe deer. This in both cases has been substantiated by the finding of their pellets, which contained the discarded bones of such animals. These owls are sexually mature by around two years old. They normally lay two to four eggs, which are incubated for about 60 days.

Similar to the tawny owl, the eagle owl is a very upright perching bird. It has a very subtle call, 'oo', which seems very subdued for such a giant of a bird.

This owl has been a favourite with bird owners in the past, and is still obtainable from some of the larger pet stores and pet dealers.

The ideal way of keeping such birds is in large aviaries outdoors, and preferably in pairs. Ideally they require live food such as mice and rats, but they will take dead food, which can be obtained through pet shops and dealers. Feed owls daily and, if using frozen food, ensure it is defrosted fully and warmed before giving it to them.

The daily thick liquid excrement left by these birds is very pungent, and requires cleaning away on a regular basis. Therefore the base of the aviary should include a sandy area beneath the perching, that can be easily lifted to dispose of any excrement. This should be carried out on a daily basis. If these birds are kept indoors, which is not recommended, they can become very anti-social in regard to the strong smell from their liquid droppings.

The aviary needs to be large enough for the birds to be able to fly, and should also include a shallow pool for their daily bathing. The roof, back, and sides of the aviary should be partly covered, to enable them to shelter from inclement weather, and suitable nesting areas included either in the form of a hollowed-out piece of tree trunk, or a suitable box large enough for the birds to get into and turn around in. For example, a wooden nesting box for a pair of eagle owls would be 1m long, 1m high, and 60cm wide with a half front and solid roof. This would allow both birds access at any time.

DISEASES OF BIRDS

Like all creatures, birds suffer from various forms of sickness, and positive identification of any ailment is imperative. One easy way of identifying problems is observing the change in colour of their droppings.

Below I have listed some changes to look for when examining the droppings (please note this is only a guide):

a. When yellow or cinnamon replaces the white in the droppings, this may indicate a liver or kidney disorder.

b. Grey, replacing white in the droppings, occurs with minor ailments, but can also be present in kidney disorders or neoplasia (tumours or growths).

c. Green, replacing white in droppings, could indicate crop necrosis (a limited portion of tissue dies), hepatitis (inflammation of the liver), starvation, or psittacosis (a disease of parrots causing respiratory problems) which can be harmful to humans.

d. Black droppings can indicate complete starvation with no water or food, especially if the droppings are small in quantity.

e. Diarrhoea normally indicates enteritis, to which most birds can be susceptible; organisms responsible for this state can be salmonella (a serious form of food poisoning), E.Coli (bacterial infections mostly in the gut), and coccidiosis, which is caused by a form of parasite.

Some other forms of illness and their probable causes

1. Fits, tremors, ataxia (the loss of power governing movements), and paralysis.
   These generally occur when the brain has been affected by infection, poisoning, nutritional deficiency, or head injuries.

2. Debility. The bird looks off colour, sitting still on the ground with feathers fluffed up, not eating properly and not as alert as usual. The cause can be one of a number of diseases, such as viral or bacterial infection, neoplasia, thyroid insufficiency, or nutritional deficiency. The latter can be helped by providing extra protein, such as cows' milk diluted with water 50:50, given daily. Also the bird should be kept warm at 27°C (80°F), in a suitable hospital cage.

3. The eyes. The most common ailments of the eyes are blepharitis (inflammation of the eyelids) and conjunctivitis (inflammation of the conjunctiva, which is the membrane covering the front of the eye).The two often occur together.
Causes vary from foreign bodies in the eye, vitamin A deficiency, or a viral infection such as variola (a series of fevers of animals and man, in which the skin erupts forming what are known as 'pocks'), herpes virus, or on rare occasions ornithosis, which affects the respiratory tract. Vitamin A deficiency can be rectified by suitable feeding, but in the case of a viral infection, there is no satisfactory treatment.
4. Broken limbs. These are more likely in wild birds. The limbs will set very quickly, so the main problem is that of keeping the limb in position whilst healing occurs. Splints are best for legs, but wings are difficult to align correctly, and to keep in place.
To give the affected bones a chance of setting properly, the tips of the wings should be stuck together with adhesive tape, whilst the shoulder joints are kept into the body by tapes going right round and joining at the point of the breast. The break itself is very difficult to keep in position. Although vets will not normally treat wild birds, they should be able to advise you on how to carry out these procedures.

HELP IN LOOKING AFTER YOUR BIRDS

Where is my nearest Society? Someone has made a noise complaint! How do I get planning permission? Where is my nearest Avian Vet? My parrot is dying on its perch, what can I do about it?

The work of the National Council for Aviculture covers all these matters, and represents the interests of all bird keepers at local, national and European levels. It is often instrumental in forming laws that will affect your hobby. The Council is also a member of 'PAW' (Partnership for Action Against Wildlife Crime), and runs courses in Aviary Management. Junior membership is free. See List of Useful Contacts.

CAGING OF BIRDS

The construction of cages and aviaries is best carried out by those people who are experienced in this type of work. Often one hears of people

Aviary*

designing and building their own, only to find that an animal escapes, or they have rodent infestation, or the materials have been too delicate for the weather. My own company, MAMAC Animal Consultants, deals with many enquiries about such problems, which was the main reason for creating the company originally.

However, many cages built by amateur bird keepers are sufficiently strong and secure, and have been designed to incorporate special needs for a particular bird, and their designs fit in with their surroundings, although the finish may not be to a professional standard. So what? This does not really matter, especially if the construction is outdoors, as many rugged structures fit in well with natural surroundings. But my best advice is: get advice.

The cost of building can also be inhibiting, especially if a professional is employed, whose time is paid for, whereas your time is your own and there is always satisfaction in building something yourself.

It is important to select a suitable site, away from direct winds and extremes of weather. If this is not possible, then screening should be supplied to protect the construction and its inhabitants. This could be in the form of small trees (conifers make good windbreaks), or of plastic sheeting fitted to the sides of the construction.

Some form of material should also be used to cover part of the roof, to help protect against rain, although most birds do enjoy a shower or two to help them in their grooming.

Depending on the species of bird kept, a bird room or box should be fitted on to the end of the construction to make sleeping quarters or nesting areas, which may have to be heated. Some birds will naturally build nests outside, provided suitable 'furniture' and building materials have been put into the cage. This could be in the form of trees, perches, shrubbery, or other foliage.

The floor of the cage should be designed to give as wide a range of terrain as possible, for example a grassed area, a sanded area, a shallow pool, a shingle area around the pool, a leafy area for foraging for insects etc. Sand may also be put under the perches to facilitate cleaning.

Many ideas can be incorporated into a cage, but it must never be over-done, as the birds still need a lot of space to be able to fly.

*Available from Southern Aviaries, Uckfield, Sussex

Over a period of time, the soil in the cage may have to be replaced, due to constant fouling by droppings. One method of overcoming this problem is to build two cages and leave one dormant for one year, then transfer the birds to it for the next year, and so on. This is not always preferable, since an empty aviary does seem to be a waste of space. Separate summer and winter quarters, within the same structure, might be the answer. Maybe during the winter the birds can use the bird room affixed to the side of the structure, and then be let out into the flight once the main structure has been thoroughly cleaned and its areas replenished. This will help the soil to reorganise itself.

Naturally, daily cleaning of the cage should not be neglected. To ease cleaning, concrete has been used in the past for the floors of aviaries, but it has been proved to be unsuitable. Accidentally falling onto such a base has proved fatal to birds, so a softer material should be used. A natural one is more beneficial and, of course, looks better.

A light-looking construction is appropriate to an aviary. It has been the custom, in the past, to use heavy timbers, but for most structures about 4m in length, 50mm square timber is sufficient. When the framework is complete and the wire is then stapled on, it will prove to be a very strong construction. Naturally, if large birds such as eagles are being kept, then a more robust cage will be appropriate.

It must also be borne in mind that parrots can and will be destructive, so giving sufficient materials in the cage for 'demolition' is imperative. This usually stops the animal from picking at the framework of the aviary. Normally, the wood will outlive the wire, provided it is treated annually with a non-toxic preservative.

When constructing the sleeping/nest box shelter, remember that most birds will not enter anywhere which is dark, or too small, or not tall enough. By covering all or part of the roof of the shelter with translucent sheeting, you will give enough light for the birds, and will create a natural night and day situation.

Providing various feeding areas in a mixed aviary is important, so that all birds can get a fair share of food. When housing is for just one pair, then one site is usually sufficient.

A decent-size aviary with small adjoining shelter, for a mixed collection of birds, will cost in the region of £200 ($290) minimum. In addition to this, heating may be required during the winter period, especially if small tropical birds are to be kept, and this could cost a further £5 ($7) per week. Feeding is dependent on the species of bird being kept, and how many. One 12kg sack of seed will cost from £9 to £16 ($13–23), depending on variety. Fruit prices depend on time of year and availability.

When keeping a selection of different birds in the same aviary, it is possible to intermix seed eaters, with insect eaters, with fruit eaters. As an example, say you have built an aviary 4m long, 2m high and 1.5m wide, with a heated shed 2m high, 2m long and 1.5m wide. This would be a suitable size for keeping, say, one pair of fruit doves, one pair of breeding Bengalese finches, one pair of breeding Chinese painted quail, one pair of breeding water rail and a pair of breeding zosterops. To start with, the aviary would probably look a bit under-stocked, but, because of regular breedings, it would soon start to fill.

By doing it this way, the possibility of infighting amongst the different species would be minimised, although introducing other birds at a later date may encourage it.

Having few stock to begin with will give better opportunity to develop the aviary terrain with grassed areas, sanded areas and water features, and any shrubs etc. planted will get the chance to root and grow. From my experience, once an aviary has been landscaped it takes a little time for the whole of it to settle and become established. There may be occasions when topping up sand or gravel is essential.

Typical mixed species aviary constructed from reclaimed timber

One aviary which I personally had in my house in London was actually in one of the sitting rooms. It measured 4.5m long in an 'L' shape, 1m deep and 3.5m high. This was landscaped with rocks, a sanded area, a peated area, many plants and perches, and a pool. Several nesting sites were also placed around the aviary.

It eventually contained a pair of Chinese painted quail, a pair of fruit pigeons, two species of whydah (weaver birds), a pair of Pekin robins, two pairs of zosterops, three pairs of waxbills and two pairs of finches. This aviary worked very well, the birds seemed to be very happy and bred, and, because of being indoors, needed no extra heating.

The following page reflects a cross section of the pet trade in the UK, and the USA as a comparison. On average the prices of most species are identical in both countries, at the current exchange rate of $1.43 to £1.

Many of these prices can be drastically reduced by looking in the various bird magazines and weekly papers for private sales. The *Cage and Aviary Birds* paper, that is published every Thursday, contains a selection of trade advertisements as well as private ads for the sale of birds and other animals. *Bird Talk*, published in the States, is another such paper. Joining one or more of the many bird clubs and societies, and meeting other members, can be advantageous to acquiring important information and knowledge, as well as possible contacts for purchasing home-bred birds.

Great Blue Turaco

It must always be remembered that anyone in Britain purchasing any wild bird or other wild animal should contact the local authority to obtain a licence. By writing to the: Department of the Environment (Wildlife Division), Tollgate House, Houlton Street, Bristol BS2 9DJ, it is possible to obtain a full list of animals covered by the Dangerous Wild Animals Act (1976).

SAMPLE OF PET SHOP BIRD PRICES

Parrots & Parakeets etc.	UK £	USA $
Blue and Gold macaws	1150.00 pr	1700.00 pr
Green Wing macaws	1150.00 pr	1700.00 pr
Blue Cheeked amazons	450.00 each	650.00 each
Umbrella cockatoo	635.00 each	1000.00 each
Celestial parakeets	45.00 pr	65.00 pr
Pennant parakeets	125.00 pr	180.00 pr
Quaker parrots	120.00 pr	175.00 pr
African Grey parrots	675.00 each	800.00 each
Nyasa lovebirds	80.00 pr	115.00 pr
Red Faced lovebirds	220.00 pr	315.00 pr
Abyssinian lovebirds	120.00 pr	175.00 pr
Black Cheeked lovebirds	45.00 pr	65.00 pr
Black Masked lovebirds	35.00 pr	50.00 pr

Finches etc.		
Blue Capped waxbills	15.00 pr	20.00 pr
Sundervalls waxbills	12.00 pr	18.00 pr
Blue Billed mannikins	9.50 pr	14.00 pr
Cordon Bleu waxbills	19.50 pr	30.00 pr
Desert Bullfinches	45.00 pr	65.00 pr
Hill mynahs	145.00 each	210.00 each
Bank mynahs	40.00 pr	60.00 pr
Swainson's toucans	995.00 pr	1400.00 pr
Red Vented bulbuls	35.00 pr	50.00 pr
Virginia cardinals	260.00 pr	370.00 pr
Peacocks	100.00 pr	150.00 pr
Canaries from	15.00 each	20.00 each
Zebra finches from	7.00 each	10.00 each

6
REPTILES (Reptilia)

Reptiles are vertebrates which are poikilothermic, i.e. have a body temperature which is comparable to the surrounding air temperature. In other words they are cold-blooded. They are adapted to life on the land, although some do live in water, but are air-

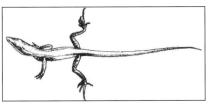

Green lizard

breathing. The skin usually has visible scales and none have fur, feather or hair. They lay amniotic eggs, i.e. eggs filled with a fluid similar to that found in a bird's egg. The embryo forms in the egg until hatching.

Reptiles are classed in four orders:

1. Chelonia – turtles, tortoises, terrapins
2. Rhynocephalia – tuatara (a species of primitive reptile)
3. Squamata – lizards, snakes
4. Crocodilia – gavial, crocodiles, alligators

These four orders are separated into two groups:

• One group has limbs, rigid jaws, eyelids in most, visible eardrums, and several rows of ventral scales. For example, the crocodile.

• The second group has no limbs, a wide gape, no eyelids and just stares, no external ear, and most have one row of ventral scales. For example, the snake.

Tortoise

Reptiles are either carnivorous or omnivorous, and swallow their food whole or in chunks.

Tortoises find their food by smell. They prefer leafy grasses, cabbage, lettuce, clover, dandelion, soft fruits such as tomato and orange, boiled egg and canned dog food. The food can be sprinkled with oatmeal, and mineral and vitamin supplement.

Iguanas, agamids and skinks prefer such foods as tomato, peach, orange, insects, boiled egg, chopped mice, tinned dog food. The food can be sprinkled with a proprietary baby cereal, and a mineral and vitamin supplement.

Small lizards prefer live insect food, earthworms, raw eggs and small mice. The food can be dusted with mineral and vitamin supplement powders.

Chameleon

Geckos and chameleons prefer live insects such as crickets and locusts. The food can be dusted with mineral and vitamin supplement powders, or, better still, feed the insects on the powder before feeding the reptiles.

Larger lizards prefer small mice, rats, chopped meat, dog food, and raw egg. The food can be dusted with mineral and vitamin supplement powders.

Small crocodilia prefer earthworms, shrimps, strips of meat. The food can be dusted with mineral and vitamin supplement powders.

Bigger crocodilia prefer fish, mice, rats, chicks. The fish should have a calcium supplement added.

Large crocodilia prefer large joints of meat which they can tear chunks from, and fish. Again the fish should have a calcium supplement added.

Turtles and terrapins prefer fish, shrimps, earthworms, locusts. The food can be sprinkled with mineral and vitamin supplement powders. There are also pelleted foods, which are readily available from good pet shops, and make feeding easier.

Sailfin lizard

Small snakes prefer invertebrates, whereas large snakes prefer mice, rats, chicks, chickens, rabbits. There is one snake which prefers eggs and that is the Dasypeltis scaber (Egg-eating snake).

Some reptiles will feed twice a week such as the smaller snakes, but the larger snakes and crocodilia may be fed once a week. Tortoises may take food daily during the warmer months, and if kept indoors during the winter, may also take a little food. Those which are kept in a cold garage or similar building will normally hibernate for the winter period, requiring no food at all, although it is advisable to leave water down in case the animal wakes up during the hibernation period.

Boa constrictor

Always offer food in the evening. Normally, live food is taken head first and swallowed whole. Don't forget to remove any left-over food the next morning.

Reptiles can be difficult to feed, especially when you are trying to introduce dead food, and if the reptile is newly imported. If it fails to eat on several occasions, then either raise the temperature in the cage by about 5°C, or give it a warm bath to increase its metabolism to induce feeding; if all fails consult a veterinary surgeon. The animal can be force-fed, but this must be the last resort and should be carried out by a veterinary surgeon, or someone else who is conversant with reptiles.

> "On no occasion must you touch the rats or the mice and then handle the snakes," I said to one of the junior staff at my zoo. James went into the storeroom and proceeded to clean out the mice and rats. Without washing his hands he picked up the pythons' food and opened the door to their cage. Immediately one of the animals lunged forward and took James's hand into its mouth. It took half an hour and a screwdriver to tease its mouth open to release James's hand. It then took another two hours to run him to hospital for treatment and a tetanus injection. Needless to say, James never did it again.

SNAKES (Serpentes)

In Britain we only have three species of snake, (and there are none at all in Ireland): the Adder (Vipera berus), also called the viper and the only poisonous one; the Grass snake (Natrix natrix); and the Smooth snake

Common adder

(Coronella austriaca). They look as different from one another as chalk and cheese. Many people are so alarmed when they see one, that they panic. If you take your time and observe the snake calmly, you should not end up killing a grass snake needlessly or picking up an adder because you thought it was harmless!

First of all it depends on where you are, as to which snake you may see. You can come across an adder anywhere in Britain. Grass snakes are common too, except north of the Scottish border counties. However, you would be very lucky to find a smooth snake, as they are so rare, and there are only small numbers of them living on the sandy heaths of England's southern counties.

Adders vary in their base colour, which tends to go from whitish to brown, but the broad dark zigzag down the back of the snake is unmistakable. Less obvious in the heat of the moment, is a dark V or X on top of its head.

Grass snakes are generally longer than adders, and are olive green. They usually have vertical dark bars along the sides of the body, but never the adder's bold zigzag.

Smooth snakes are mainly grey to reddish brown, with small delicate dark spots, often in two rows along the back.

If ever you see a snake, treat it with respect and leave it alone, as even the grass snake can unsociably secrete a liquid which gives off a foul smell, if the animal is picked up.

Many non-poisonous snakes make fascinating pets. Although they do not show affection in the same way as a cat or dog, they have interesting habits that will amuse you. If you have never kept a snake before, then the following may be of use.

Snakes should have plenty of room to be able to move about, and to climb.

A large aquarium, which will cost around £20 ($28), is suitable to keep a small snake, but some small snakes grow into large snakes, and this must be borne in mind when first acquiring your animal. An Indian or Burmese python reaches 5–6 metres when fully grown, so a very large cage should be built. A suggested size is 2m long, 2m wide and 2.5m high, and it should be made out of glass and plywood, and have no places where the animal can attempt to escape, which could damage it. This will cost in the region of £60 ($85), taking into account the cost of glass.

Python species

The floor of the cage can be covered in bark strippings, to a reasonable depth of 7–10cm.

Suitable shelves should be put into the cage, large enough for the animal to be able to coil upon.

Make a pond, again large enough for the snake to be able to submerge the whole of its body. Snakes not only drink water, they also like to lie in it, especially after a heavy meal.

Large branches, pre-cleaned, can be placed in the cage for the animal to climb on, but no living plants should be introduced, as these can harbour fungi that could have a detrimental effect on the animal.

You can heat the cage by using tubular heaters, but these must either be encased in wooden boxes with many small ventilation holes, or covered all round in a very fine mesh, about 25cm from the heater itself. Either way, the covering must be firmly secured to the underside of the shelves, or to the wall at floor level. All wires should also be covered in trunking. If the animal comes into contact with the heater, then it will coil its body around it, and seriously burn itself. These heaters start from £12 ($17). A good temperature for Indian Pythons (Python molurus molurus) or Burmese pythons (Python molurus bivittatus) is around 29°C (84°F). Normally it is Burmese pythons that you will find for sale in pet shops, although they both look similar to the untrained eye. Remember that pythons do not like the damp, so it is important to keep the temperature constant, although at night it can be reduced slightly to imitate the natural environment.

Clean the cage regularly, at least once a week, taking out any droppings or sloughed skin. Shedding the skin happens more frequently with young snakes, and an adult may only shed once a year. Placing suitable 'furniture' in the cage helps snakes to shed. They will rub themselves against branches or rocks, to get themselves started, and then hook the old skin on to a branch and pull themselves out of it.

As stated before, feeding can be once a week especially for the larger snakes, but usually the animal will tell you when it is hungry, by actively moving about near the door or usual feeding area.

Snakes do better when not handled too often, and they do like to hide, so some form of hideaway box or cave made from concrete should be provided. This will enable an animal to choose its desired body temperature.

Diseases in snakes are rare if good management and husbandry takes place. With freshly imported animals, there is always the chance that parasites may be present in the form of ticks. These are found lying just under the scales, and can be removed with an alcohol, although it is advisable to ask a veterinary surgeon to remove them, as, if the head of the tick is left in the animal, this can present further problems which could lead to infection. Examples of some diseases follow on page 66.

Garter snakes (Thamnophis sirtalis), which are another species obtainable from pet shops, do not need such a large enclosure, and can be kept in a large aquarium, costing £10–20 ($14–28). The floor should be covered with gravel to a depth of 5cm, with a hide box, water bowl and other rock formations. Maintain a temperature of 25°C, using heater pads under the aquarium.

The sexing of snakes can be difficult, but one technique is noting the shape of the tail. Normally, with pythons, the male has a long tail with swellings at the base, which can easily be seen. The female has a shorter tail, which tapers.

Mating of pythons takes place during February and March in the wild, and the eggs (15–50) are laid two to five months later. The eggs then hatch some 60–65 days later.

LIZARDS (Sauria)

Collared lizard

Lizards require more space than the snakes, as, being a more active species of reptile, they need room to run and climb. The small, agile lizards have well developed legs, and long tails from which they can shed part if caught by a predator, or if mishandled. The piece of tail that is left will grow again, but will not attain the same length as the original, or have the same colouring.

These lizards require a large aquarium (vivarium) with gravel for the floor, dressed with cork bark, rocks and branches. Heating should be in the region of 25–30°C (77°–86°F), which can be achieved with under-tank heat pads and spotlights. A water bowl should be provided to drink from, and the vivarium should be very secure to prevent escape.

BASILISKS

The basilisks are a group of arboreal (tree dwelling) iguana lizards, found in Mexico and Ecuador. There are four known species: the common, the banded, the red-headed and the green.

Plumed basilisk

They have been nicknamed the 'Jesus Christ lizard' due to the fact they can 'walk' on water. Another interesting name for this creature is the 'cockatrice'. By all accounts their name comes from the mythological basilisk which was a reptile with deadly breath and a deadly gaze. They were said (fancifully) to have been bred by reptiles from chicken eggs.

Basilisks live in the trees of the tropical rain forests as well as in rock formations. The adults have impressive crests along their backs and bony casques (helmets) on their heads, which are much more prominent on the males. Their tails are long and whip-like, and their bodies tall yet narrow. The females are much smaller than the males. They grow to 60–75cm long but most of that is the tail.

They are diurnal (active by day) creatures and feed on crickets, grasshoppers, spiders, worms and small mammals, which they mostly find in and on the branches of trees. They have been known to eat some fruit.

Although they have four very long legs, they are one of the few animals that will run on two legs. Whilst running, they hold their tails upright to aid balance. Like other lizards, the basilisk can lose part of the tail through predators, fighting etc. and when this happens it can prevent the animal from raising itself up on its back legs to run, as the balance is lost. Basilisks are very fast runners on land as well as over the surface of water. They have fringes on their toes that trap bubbles of air below the surface of the water, which helps to support them. Being very good swimmers they will then dive into the water and make their escape. This gives them an advantage over any predator that may be chasing them. The adult of the species has been known to reach speeds of up to 12 kilometres (7 miles) per hour on land. This speed is normally over a short distance. It has also been documented that young basilisks can cover up to 20 metres on the water surface, especially when being chased.

They are egg-laying reptiles, laying up to 15 eggs at a time, and these take up to 80 days to incubate. The female, once mated, will dig a shallow hole in the moist ground to lay her eggs in, then cover them with dirt. That is her job done, and she will leave the eggs to their own devices.

Once the youngsters have hatched, they become self sufficient, catching and eating insects for themselves, after climbing up into the safety of the trees.

The only predators the basilisks have in the wild are large snakes such as the boa constrictor, and some larger birds such as the quetzal.

Gecko

GECKOS (Gekkonidae)

It is difficult to estimate the number of species of gecko, but different organisations suggest there are between 400 and 700. Many of these can be found in Southeast Asia, India, Australia and the East Indies, but only a few species are suitable as house pets. They are a family of insectivorous, mostly nocturnal lizards, in which the eye has a vertical pupil and spectacle, therefore no eyelid. The skin is soft, with sparse horny bumps. The toes usually have crosswise rows of hooked membrane for adhesion to flat surfaces. The tail is used as a store for fat and can be cast off when the animal is threatened. Being a nocturnal creature, it is less interesting to observe during the day.

Geckos enjoy a dry, warm environment. They especially need to be contained and not let loose within the house, as this species of lizard can be difficult to maintain and needs a good supply of live food. They require a tall style of vivarium, at least 60cm long by 30cm deep, with an escape-proof lid. The flooring within the vivarium can be a thin layer of sand with pieces of cork bark for the animal to hide under, and rocks and branches to climb and rest on. It needs to be heated to 25–30°C (77°–86°F). Because Geckos can shed part of their tail and the skin tears easily, handle them with care. They also bite.

They feed on live insects, such as the fruit fly, housefly, crickets, mealworms etc. They, like most other lizards, also require some form of vitamin D3, which can be given by introducing an ultraviolet light source in the roof of the vivarium. Without sufficient D3, which in the wild they would get from the sun, bone growth can be jeopardised as calcium levels will fail. D3 in powder form can now be obtained with a calcium lactate. This given regularly will maintain the correct levels in the animal, and so prevent any bone disorders.

When giving mealworms and crickets to geckos, it is advisable to feed the live food on a mineral and vitamin powder supplement, as this will then be passed on to the animal.

Water should be accessible at all times, and if the gecko will not drink from a dish then water should be sprinkled onto branches daily.

TORTOISES (Testudinidae)

Tortoises are not as common as they used to be, now that the importation laws have been tightened. Only a few can be imported at a time, and those that do get into the pet shops are quite expensive.

The ones usually available are those from the Mediterranean islands. They can live outdoors in this country during a warm summer, but the garden must be checked for escape routes, as these animals can climb small walls. There should be some form of shelter, as well as a water bowl supplied.

Mediterranean tortoise

During the winter, the tortoise may be hibernated or can be housed in a vivarium heated to at least 20°C (64°F). If the animal is to be hibernated, feeding should not continue after the middle of September. This is to make sure that the digestive tract is emptied before the winter sleep. During October, the tortoise should be put into a rodent-proof box, containing hay or straw, and the box wrapped in sacks (not plastic) and placed in a garage or outhouse where the temperature does not fall below 5°C (41°F).

Hibernation usually ends around the beginning of April, when the animal should be allowed to drink and bathe in warm water. Food can be offered, but it may take some time before it resumes its full diet. When the weather is again warm, it can be returned to the garden, but keep your eyes open for evening or early morning frosts that can occur.

Depending on the age of the tortoise, feeding must be correct, otherwise defects in the shell will occur. Young tortoises should be fed on a variety of foods such as chopped fruit and vegetables, animal protein (canned dog food is a suitable food, as is minced meat), mashed hard boiled eggs, sprats, and mineral and vitamin supplements given daily. SA37, available from most pet shops, is only one of many supplements available.

Adult animals, i.e. 10 years or more, will start to eat more vegetables than the younger ones. A selection of clovers, grasses, fruit and vegetables are eaten by healthy animals, provided the temperature is warm enough to stimulate an appetite.

Sexing young tortoises is difficult, but adults can be sexed by the length of the tail. The males have much longer tails than the females, and also have a concave area in the plastron, the under shell of the tortoise. The top of the shell is called the carapace.

DISEASES IN REPTILES

Abscesses
Subcutaneous (beneath the outermost layer of skin) ones are most common. They are normally blood borne and treatment must be carried out by a veterinary surgeon.

Burns
Bad management causes burns, such as the failure to protect the animal from all heat sources. Treat daily with Betadine.

Conjunctivitis
There is no conjunctival membrane, but in cases of incomplete sloughing (the shedding of the skin), an eye infection can occur. This is a sub-spectacle abscess and must only be treated by a veterinary surgeon.

Constipation
Improper diet, insufficient exercise, and being fed heavily furred rodents such as guinea pigs, tend to produce large dry masses of 'felt'.

Treat with liquid paraffin by stomach tube. A dog tube is sufficient for a python or boa, and a human tube cut down is suitable for a garter snake. Veterinary supervision must be obtained, as damage to the animal can occur if treatment is not carried out properly.

Ecdysis

Ecdysis, or sloughing, occurs in all reptiles. Small lizards and small snakes slough whole skins. Large pythons and boas slough piece-meal. Failure to shed the skin usually occurs in sick animals, areas of low humidity, or dehydration.

Treat by soaking the reptile in warm water, and using wet towelling try to take off the skin.

If eye spectacles fail to shed on snakes, remove them by lifting the edges carefully and peel them off. Never force them, and do not attempt to try this without veterinary supervision.

Ectoparasites

Ticks are the main problem; they usually come in under the scales of animals fresh from the wild, and can infect other reptiles in the same tank. If not dealt with immediately, they can cause anaemia. The only treatment is applying some form of alcohol to the ticks, and then with tweezers withdrawing them from under the scales. This should really be done by a skilled person or a veterinary surgeon, as failure to get a tick out complete can result in further problems with the animal.

Vivarium mites commonly occur through bad management. They cause irritation around the spectacles of the host animal. Isolate it in a clean vivarium immediately, while the original cage is thoroughly cleaned by hanging a vapona strip inside for a week. This should kill all mites and the subsequent hatchlings. Veterinary advice should be sought before any treatment is given.

Mouth rot

There are several identifiable symptoms. With the reptile's mouth open, look for small spots on the roof of the mouth. Also look for areas of mucous fluid or pus. Look down the throat for any signs of infection. Look at the teeth for any crusting, which in neglected cases can weld the mandible to the upper jaw, so that the animal cannot open its mouth. Also check if there is any smell from the mouth.

Treatment must be carried out by a veterinary surgeon, and normally consists of anaesthesia and removal of debris in the mouth, and the taking of swabs to diagnose the type of infection. This in turn will determine the form of treatment.

Protozoan (one-celled micro organisms) infection

Intestinal infections can cause wet cloacal voidings in reptiles. The animal will drink excessively, and treatment by stomach tube with Metronizadole should be carried out by a veterinary surgeon.

Regurgitation of stomach contents

Three main conditions may cause this:
1. Handling within about three days of feeding.
2. Temperature too low in the vivarium, which fails to cause any digestive enzyme activity.
3. Gastritis and bacteraemia (inflammation of the stomach or disease in the stomach). Death may occur within 48 hours.

Scale rot

Do not confuse this with burns. Lesions show loss of dermis (skin) and raw ulcerated patches occur. They are usually multiple, and both types of scaling are affected. Treat by taking swabs for culture, and by cleaning all lesions and applying antiseptic such as Betadine daily. Keep the animal warm and clean, preferably on paper, and give fresh drinking water.

When results of tests are known, treatment is with antibiotics. Healing can take 12 weeks or longer. Offer food after a few weeks. Naturally all the above will be carried out with the assistance of a veterinary surgeon.

Rhinoceros iguana

7
AMPHIBIANS (Amphibia)

Amphibians are divided into three orders: Urodela (the salamanders, which includes newts and sirens), Anura (the frogs and toads), and Gymnophiona (the legless caecilians).

The word amphibian comes from the Greek 'amphibios', which roughly interpreted means something with a double life, specifically one that can alternate life on land and in the water.

Amphibians can be either ovoviviparous, i.e. ones which give birth to live young, or oviparous, ones which lay eggs. Fertilised eggs can be laid singly, in clusters or in strands, but all are enclosed in a gelatinous case. Toads and frogs lay their eggs in ponds, lakes, and streams, and their larvae are known as tadpoles which are herbivorous, tearing and scraping plant material for food. Once adult they become carnivorous, living off a variety of insect life and other invertebrates. Salamander larvae on the other hand are carnivorous, and carry on accordingly into adulthood.

Common toad

Toad spawn is laid in strings, which eventually come together in double rows of gelatinous-coated black eggs, which are woven around the base of plants. These individual strings may contain up to 4,000 eggs. Many are eaten by fish, and also by waterbirds such as ducks.

Frogs lay their eggs in clusters which sink when laid, but the gelatinous substance that surrounds the eggs takes up water and swells, which causes the masses of eggs to rise to the surface of the water. The time for frog spawn to hatch and develop is dependent on temperature and food availability, and in some mountainous regions the development of the embryos may be delayed for up to twelve months.

Common newt

The most common species of British newt is the Smooth Newt (Triturus vulgaris), which start migrating to ponds, lakes and streams in early April. The males start to assume under-body colours of beautiful yellows and oranges, and develop a wavy crest which extends along the whole of the back and tail, in readiness for the breeding season. The females do not have this adornment, but normally produce up to 400 eggs during this time.

Caecilian

Caecilians look very much like earthworms, with segmental rings around their bodies, but are in fact burrowing amphibians. It can be seen from their body make-up that they are related to salamanders and frogs. They are carnivorous, having two rows of teeth on the upper jaw, and live on earthworms and termites. They give birth to live young, although some primitive species lay eggs in burrows near streams.

The tree-dwelling amphibians, such as the small delicate tree-frogs, are now available from good pet stores. These creatures are brightly coloured and are mostly nocturnal. They live in the humid tropics, so their captive environment needs to be a tall enclosure, well ventilated but very secure, planted with broad-leafed plants, which the animal will cling to and hide on, and they need high humidity. They will feed on small flying insects, such as fruit flies and small house flies.

Amphibians are reasonably easy animals to keep in captivity, but care of their habitat is very important. Being partly aquatic animals, a moist condition is imperative for them at all times.

Depending on the number of animals to be kept, the most appropriate enclosure for them is an aquarium, costing between £20 and £30 ($30–44). The larger the aquarium the better, as more interesting features can be included in the general layout, especially if a mixed collection is to be kept.

A reasonable-size pool of fresh water should be included, so they have a chance to submerge themselves or even swim, but make sure that the pool bottom slopes from a boggy area to the deeper parts, so they can easily come out of the water if need be. Plants introduced into the enclosure will make it look more natural, and will help oxygenate the water, especially if it is a large expanse.

With larger enclosures, a form of filtration unit may be included, to keep the water clean and free from impurities.

You can feed with a proprietary brand of dried food, but it is more beneficial for the animals to take live food, such as earthworms, mealworms, blowfly, fruitfly etc. Also strips of raw meat can be given, but this will eventually cloud the water if (a) the filtration unit is inefficient, or (b) the water is not changed regularly.

It is advisable to keep only amphibians of equal size, as large specimens have a habit of eating the smaller ones, even if they are of the same family.

Excess heat will kill your animals, so make sure the enclosure is well away from direct sunlight.

As already stated, amphibians require a moist environment, the reason being that they take moisture through the skin, and their bodies take oxygen from that moisture. Never handle them with dry hands. Frogs and salamanders are covered with a form of mucus which is necessary to their general health, although toads and newts do not have this mucus.

Toads and salamanders do not require a complete water environment, so their enclosure should be dressed with a good layer of earth or peat, covered partly with living moss. Any natural material of this nature will help to keep moisture in the enclosure. Plants can also be grown in the earth or peat, which will help to make the enclosure look natural and give places for the animals to hide, as will pieces of bark, rock, slate, and small flower pots on their sides buried in the earth. Make sure they are deep enough for the animal to get into completely, and to turn round. Fresh water can be put into a shallow pool, deep enough and large enough to allow the animals to submerge themselves, to keep their bodies wet. As already mentioned, ensure the pool slopes up from deep to shallow, with a platform, so that they can easily emerge from the pool and use the platform to feed from.

The enclosure itself should be sprayed with water daily, ensuring the floor material is also kept moist, but not soaking.

With any enclosure built for amphibians, a good secure meshed or glazed, well ventilated top should be supplied, to prevent them escaping. The finer the mesh, the better.

Sexing of amphibians is easy in some species, but difficult in others. It is usually better to sex an amphibian in the breeding season when, for example, the males of some newts grow crests, and are more colourful than the

Common frog

females. Certain frogs and toads develop swellings on the forelimbs, which only occurs in the males. These swellings are called 'nuptial pads'.

The life cycle of the amphibians is unlike that of any other species of vertebrate. Eggs are laid in the water, usually in the early spring for the common toads and frogs, and are called spawn. After a few days, tailed tadpoles begin to form and break free from the jelly-like spawn. As the days pass, limbs begin to grow starting with the front legs, then the back legs. Gills serve as lungs during this period, but eventually the gills disappear and the lungs take over. It is about this time that the tail disappears and the tadpole emerges from the water as a small replica of the adult. This process of change, from aquatic tadpole to land-living adult, is called metamorphosis, and takes up to two months to complete.

Axolotl

In some Mexican lakes, there is an amphibian tadpole called an Axolotl, which is a species of neotenous salamander. Neotony is when there is a slowing down of development or metamorphosis, which enables the creature to reach sexual maturity, but still remain a juvenile tadpole. Therefore an axolotl can go through the normal procedures of copulation, and breed other axolotls. If the animal continues to metamorphose, then eventually it will turn into a salamander. This will sometimes occur when water courses such as the lakes dry up, or when sufficient iodine compounds are available in the diet.

DISEASES OF AMPHIBIANS

Diseases can be kept to a minimum, if proper husbandry is carried out. One of the most common diseases, caused by bacteria, is 'red leg'. This can be brought on by stress, especially in a crowded tank, so care should be taken not to introduce too many animals into one exhibit. When 'red leg' is recognised on an animal, it must be isolated from the others, and a veterinary surgeon consulted for the proper treatment with antibiotics, although this does not always remedy the condition.

TOMATO FROGS LOOK LIKE TOMATOES!

One day a customs officer, Malcolm, who lived in my village, asked if I would accompany some of his colleagues to an address in Torquay, to identify some Tomato Frogs, which they suspected had been smuggled in from Madagascar and which were an endangered species. On arriving at the house an officer knocked on the door and it was opened by the dealer, Nick "What the hell is he doing here?" he asked, pointing at me. Malcolm said that they had brought me along to identify the frogs for them. Nick, being the stupid person he was said, "You don't need him here: Tomato Frogs are easy enough to identify, they look like tomatoes." The Customs asked Paul for entry with me and he eventually agreed. In a back room there were tanks of reptiles and amphibians around the walls, and tucked away at the bottom was a tank containing nine roundish, red frogs. The Customs asked me for a definite identification and then seized the frogs, and asked where the other three were as they had been told twelve came into the country.

"Sold them," said Nick.

"Who to?" asked Malcolm.

"I don't know," said Nick cheekily, "I just receive a letter and a cheque, box up the animals and send them, then throw away the letter and bank the cheque." Malcolm could see they were not going to get any more information out of him, so we left with the frogs. These finished up at the zoo and the Customs asked me if I did not mind being a subsidiary to the Queen's Warehouse, as they needed places to put such animals until they could be disposed of to other animal organisations or sent back to the wild.

"I don't mind," I said, "but what if Nick or his accomplices try to steal them back?"

"He doesn't know they are here and he won't find out," said Malcolm. "Anyway it will only take us a couple of weeks to get him in court, then the frogs can go."

Malcolm was true to his word as Nick was fined and his stock seized when he was found guilty as a smuggler. This did not deter him as not long after he was done again for smuggling, but this time he served a sentence in prison.

8

INSECTS (Insecta) AND SPIDERS (Arachnida)

Mention insects to some people, and the first thing is that their skin crawls, and then they tend to reach for the insect spray.

But for other people these creatures do hold a certain amount of fascination, and I have included a couple of examples which can be kept with the least amount of effort.

Some insects, such as the ant, live in tremendously complicated societies, which in many ways are very similar to our own.

As with most other animals, a good secure container or enclosure is required to prevent the them from escaping into the outside world, i.e. your living room.

Some insects can be kept in large pickle jars, although most are more suited to a small aquarium, providing a secure lid with ample ventilation is included, enough to enable sufficient air to circulate through the jar but not the inmates through your house.

Wood Ant

WOOD ANT (Formica rufa)

Ant colonies or ant farms can be bought commercially, with everything you will need, but it is much cheaper to try and start your own colony.

When starting, you must make sure that you successfully capture a queen ant with her workers, otherwise they will not breed and eventually die, although they may survive for a couple of weeks. (Ants only live to about one year old.)

Once you have found your ant nest, continue to dig downwards and you should find eggs, cocoons and larvae, along with the queen and workers. Transfer them to your jar or receptacle, and fill in the hole you have made. Once you have your ants indoors, put the container in the fridge for about an hour whilst you prepare your exhibit. Carrying out this treatment to them does no harm, but will slow the ants down before you transfer them to the final enclosure.

One simple way of ensuring that all the activities of the ants can be observed by you, is to put soil around a block of wood or brick, in the centre of your enclosure. This will keep the tunnels out to the edge of the tank and on view.

Putting in small plants, lumps of rock, pieces of bark etc. will enhance the look of your exhibit, but do remember that the ants will climb everywhere and also probably destroy any living material. Don't forget to place a small receptacle for water somewhere in the enclosure.

Once the enclosure is ready, carefully introduce your ants, then cover it in newspaper and leave it for a few days to enable the ants to begin their tunnelling. Keep the enclosure out of the sun's rays, at room temperature but away from the radiators. Moisten the earth on occasions with water, but not too much as this will make the earth soggy and mould may develop.

Feed the colony every other day with bits of fruit, bread, vegetables, cereal, seeds and also some drops of sugar water. If food is put onto a flat piece of slate or plastic, then it is simpler to remove untouched food, and makes it easier for you to see what the ants like and dislike. By this process you can add and remove foods accordingly, varying them so the ants have a lot of choice. Be careful not to overfeed them.

When looking after other animals, such as amphibians, which require an insectivorous diet, it is cheaper if you can breed your own insects. Here are a couple of examples which may be helpful.

FLIES (Dipteva)

The Common Housefly (Musca domestica) is a simple one to start with. A well secured tank or large bottle is necessary, and two or three pairs of flies. Inside the cage place pieces of kitchen roll paper soaked in milk, so

House fly

that the adult flies can deposit their eggs on them. A constant temperature of 26°C (78°F) should be maintained, to ensure the eggs hatch quickly.

Once the eggs have hatched and the maggots have formed, feed these on a mixture of yeast, sugar and bran, with ground-up rodent pellets. One part of sugar, to two parts of yeast, to six parts of bran, to four parts of ground rodent pellets, should be sufficient. This must be put into the enclosure as carefully as possible, so as not to allow your flies to escape.

The Fruit Fly (Drosophilia melanogaster) is another simple insect to breed, and it is ideal for feeding smaller animals such as tree frogs.

An empty washed and dried large coffee jar is ideal for the breeding

Fruit fly

of these creatures. Into the jar place a piece of kitchen towel, stood upright, and put in some over-ripe fruit, especially banana. Place your adults into the jar, and stretch a piece of muslin or something similar across the opening, and secure with an elastic band. A constant temperature of 25°C (76°F) should be maintained. The eggs are laid on the paper, and, when the maggots form, they feed off the fruit. Within 13 days from laying the eggs, the flies emerge and are ready to be fed to your animals.

TARANTULAS (Theraphosidae)

Eight legs, two palps (jointed appendages at the front of the animal used to collect and hold prey), two fangs, and carries its skeleton on the outside of the body. This is the general description of the spider family.

The number of tarantulas available from pet shops, is becoming unlimited. The Red-kneed tarantula (Euthalus smithii) originally from Mexico, is the most common species to be found.

This species grows to around 12.5cm, the females usually being larger than the males. The sexing is difficult as both look alike, that is until the male reaches maturity. It is only then, around five years of age, that the male grows hooks on its front legs, which does not occur in the female.

Tarantula

The male lives to about six years of age, yet the females can live to around twelve years. On occasions the female may eat the male after mating, if he is not quick enough to get away. The reason for this is that the female must obtain protein to feed her eggs, and the male is the nearest food source at the time.

Tarantulas feed on insects such as moths, butterflies, crickets, locusts etc., but do on occasions eat other spiders and also young vertebrates such as baby mice. In captivity, they are mainly fed on crickets, which are bred for the purpose.

Tarantulas are easy to keep, and do not require large enclosures. Most species require a steady warmth of 21–24°C (70°–76°F).

Cricket

The cage itself can be a glass tank, costing around £10 ($15), with a sandy floor about 2.5cm deep, dressed with rocks and pieces of bark, to give places for the animal to hide. This form of caging does not suit all species, as some come from more humid regions such as the tropical rain forests.

Tarantulas do not normally spin a web, as do our own house and garden spiders, but lay a silk on the floor of the cage, which is linked to rocks etc., and the spider will use this to slow down any unfortunate insect that comes its way, and also use it for the shedding of its skeleton.

All spiders have to shed their outer skin, the exoskeleton, to be able to grow and also to replace any lost limbs. If a spider does lose a leg, then a new one will grow, maybe not fully on the first shed, but it will certainly be full-grown on the second. The shedding of the skin, ecdysis, may only occur once a year for an adult spider, but will occur several times per year for young spiderlings, which grow very rapidly in their first twelve months after birth.

Ecdysis is very interesting to watch, as the spider will turn itself onto its back, and the carapace will then split open. The spider then draws its body out and leaves behind its skeleton. On emergence, the 'new' spider is wet, and has to dry before it can start to move and feed. This can be the most vulnerable time for the spider in its wild environment, as it is opportune prey for many of its predators, such as the Raccoon.

Although Red-kneed tarantulas carry a venom, it is not as powerful to a human as we are led to believe. The 'bite' is painful when the fangs are pushed into the skin, but the venom injected has about the same toxicity as from a bee or wasp.

Some of the smaller tarantulas such as the Black Widow, Trap Door spider, Jockey spider and Wolf spiders, can and have been known to be lethal to man. Although serums are available, they are not always at hand when needed, especially if one is wandering into the outback of Australia, or delving into the jungles of South America, but it is not an every-day event that someone is seriously bitten by a spider, in fact quite rare.

Tarantulas can go for long periods without food, but like other animals always require water. This, in the wild, they would get from the morning dew. In captivity they will drink quite happily from a small bowl.

Mating takes place once a year. Both male and female face each other and stand on their back legs, then come together for copulation.

Around 200 eggs are laid in a silk cocoon, and it is normal for them all to hatch. In captivity this can present a problem, as being carnivorous the young spiderlings will commence to eat each other, if they are not separated into their own little tanks or containers. At this stage they feed on fruit flies and young house flies.

In America, the Red-kneed tarantula is a favourite pet with youngsters, and here in the UK they are becoming more popular. The importation of this species is now banned, as the pet trade has exhausted supplies and the animal is now becoming rare in Mexico. By careful management, this species should be able to recover, as it is unnecessary to take any more from the wild. The many which are now being bred in captivity are supplying the pet trade with its needs.

Locust, an ideal food for small monkeys
and some amphibians and birds

9

PRIMATES
(A General Overview)

There are three different families of monkey:

- The MARMOSETS and TAMARINS (Callitrichidae) of which there are 21 species.
- The CAPUCHIN-LIKE monkeys (Cebidae) of which there are 30 species.
- The OLD WORLD monkeys (Cercopithecidae) of which there are 45 species.

In many classifications the primates are grouped into two sub-orders: the Anthropoidea which includes the Old and New World monkeys, apes, and humans, and the Prosimii comprising the more primitive lemurs from Madagascar, lorises and tarsiers.

MARMOSETS AND TAMARINS

These are to be found in south Central America and the northern half of South America. Their habitat is chiefly the tropical rain forest, and they are also found in other forests.

The smallest is the Pygmy marmoset (Callithrix pygmaea pygmaea) which measures 19cm body and head length, with a 19cm tail, and the largest is the Lion Tamarin (Leontopithecus rosalia rosalia), which measures 40cm in body and head length, with a 38cm tail.

Pygmy marmoset

All marmosets' and tamarins' coats are fine and silky, many of the species having ear-tufts, manes or crests.

In captivity, these animals can live up to twelve years of age, and will produce 1–2 young, twice a year. Twins are the normal birth. The gestation period is 130–170 days, depending on the species.

Fruit and insects make up the major part of their diet, but some species of marmoset take gums and saps from trees. The marmoset is adapted to tear away the bark with its very sharp claws. True monkeys have nails and soft fleshy pads, similar to the human hand.

Nectar from flowers also makes up the diet of some marmosets and tamarins.

The main difference between the marmoset and the tamarin is the dentition. See the following chapter, on their care and management in captivity.

CAPUCHIN-LIKE MONKEYS (Cebus)

The capuchin-like monkeys are found from Mexico, south through South America to Paraguay, northern Argentina and south Brazil.

Their habitat is mostly in tropical and subtropical evergreen forests.

Sizes range from the Squirrel monkey with 30cm body and head length and a 35cm tail (Saimiri sciureus sciureus), to the largest, Woolly Spider monkey (Brachyteles arachnoides), 60cm body and head length with a 74cm tail.

Their coats vary from white, yellow, red to brown, and black, with patterning normally around the head. This family of monkey can live to around 25 years of age and normally produce one offspring each year, the gestation period being 120–225 days, depending on the species.

Their food varies between fruits, insects, leaves and seeds, and other mammals.

All have tails, of which some are prehensile and are used as a fifth limb.

Within this family is the only nocturnal monkey, the 'night monkey' or Douroucouli.

Squirrel monkey

OLD WORLD MONKEYS

This family includes the Guenons, Macaques, Baboons, Colobus and the Leaf Monkeys.

They are found throughout the lowlands of Asia, including the northern parts of Japan and Tibet, north Africa in one isolated area, and most of South Africa.

Saki monkey

Their habitats range from the snow-capped mountains to the rain forests, and from the savannah to the brush of the outback.

They vary in size from 34cm body and head length with a 35cm tail, Talapoin (Cercopithecus talapoin talapoin), to the largest 69cm body and head length with a short tail of 90mm, Drill (Papio leucophaeus leucophaeus), and Mandrill (Papio sphynx).

Their coats are long, dense and silky, and in some species the males also have manes or capes. Colour is varied, and brighter in the forest-dwelling species.

Their gestation period is between 155 and 185 days depending on the species, and normally they have one offspring. They can live up to 35 years of age, again depending on the species.

Their diets vary from fruit, insects, leaves, seeds, nuts, to other mammals.

All have short tails compared to body length, and these are non-prehensile (i.e. cannot be used to grasp by wrapping around an object).

The Colobus and Leaf monkeys differ from the other 'true monkeys' by their sizes. These range from 48cm body and head length with a 63.5cm tail (Olive colobus) up to 78cm body and head length with a tail of over 1m (Hanuman langur).

Their gestation period is 140–220 days, depending on species, and normally they have one offspring. They attain an age of 20 years on average.

Their diet contains a high input of leaves, as well as fruit and animal protein.

Barbary ape

APES

There are two families of ape.

- The GIBBONS or LESSER APES (Hylobatidae), of which there are 13 species.
- The CHIMPANZEES, ORANG-UTAN and GORILLA (Pongidae) of which there are 4 species.

They are distributed from Eastern India to South China, then south through South East Asia to the Malay Peninsula, Sumatra, Java, Borneo, and in West and Central Africa. Their habitat is mainly rain forest, but also woodland and savannah.

Gibbon

The **Gibbons** are the only apes that have developed powerful abilities to propel themselves through the trees, by using their upper limbs. The other apes, although having long limbs, do not have this attribute.

Their climbing ability is second to none, as all four feet can hold on independently, therefore giving full control to the animal when climbing.

The Gibbons measure 65cm body and head length in most species, with the exception of the Siamang which measures about 1m in body and head length. Apes do not have tails.

Their gestation period is 210–250 days, and they usually have one offspring. They can live to a good 25 years of age. Like the monkeys, their diet is omnivorous.

Chimpanzees are the apes which are seen most in zoos and other animal collections. They are endangered in the wild, and are bred in the zoos for, hopefully, reintroduction. The position now is that none can be taken from the wild for any captive state, except for those being bred in the wild state.

There are two species of chimpanzee, the Common and the Pygmy (Bonobo).

The Common comes from West and Central Africa. They live in the rain forest, woodland and savannah, also in open areas where they may search for food.

They measure 1m in body and head length. The coat is normally black with a short white beard, also in the females, and they have a pinkish bare face.

They can live up to 45 years, and normally have one youngster per year. The gestation period is 230–240 days.

Common chimpanzee

The Pygmy comes from Central Africa. Its habitat is solely in the humid forest.

They measure 75cm body and head length. The coat is black and they also have a black face. The hair projects sideways on the head, unlike that of the Common, but their lifespan and gestation periods are the same.

The **Orang-Utan** comes from North Sumatra and Borneo. They live in both the lowlands and the hilly tropical rain forest.

They measure over 1m in height and can weigh up to 90kgs. The coat is long, coarse, red hair, ranging from bright orange in the youngsters, to brown or maroon in old adults.

Their gestation period is 260–270 days, and they normally have one youngster. They can live to 35 years of age.

The **Gorilla** is the largest of the apes. They come from Central Africa and live in tropical secondary forest.

There are three races of gorilla, the Western Lowland, Eastern Lowland and the Mountain.

They measure about 1.7m in height and can weigh up to 182kgs. Their coats are black to brown/grey, with a silvery white saddle on the males.

The Mountain gorilla has longer hair on the arms, much longer teeth, and shorter arms.

Gestation of all races is about the same as the Orang-utan, 260–270 days, and they normally have one youngster. They also can live to around 35 years of age, in captivity.

Western Lowland gorilla

10

MARMOSETS AND TAMARINS
(Care and Management in Captivity)

Marmosets and tamarins can be distinguished from each other on the basis of their dentition. Marmosets have lower jaw canines and incisors of similar length (short tusked), whereas the tamarins' lower jaw canines are longer than the lower jaw incisors (long tusked); they protrude more and are seen to be dangerous, and for this reason tamarins are covered by the Dangerous Wild Animal Act.

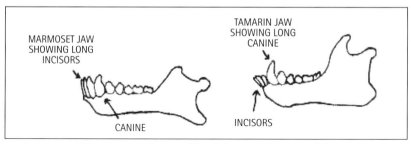

MARMOSET JAW
SHOWING LONG
INCISORS

CANINE

TAMARIN JAW
SHOWING LONG
CANINE

INCISORS

Because of the greater demand for this type of pet, and the unfortunate misunderstanding of their care and management, many marmosets are dying from neglect and ignorance.

Both marmosets and tamarins can be found throughout the deciduous and evergreen South American forests, both primary and secondary. These are the world's smallest monkeys; most are squirrel-sized, having forward-facing eyes, long tails, clawed digits, and heads that can rotate through 180° in either direction. Most species inhabit lower forest tree layers, mainly in the smaller shrubs and thinner twigs, where heavier monkeys cannot venture.

The family name of marmosets and tamarins is Callitrichidae, which actually means 'beautiful hair'. This naturally refers to the varied and spectacular patterns of the hair, throughout the group. The largest 'callitrichids' are the Lion tamarins, of which there are three species, and their weight averages 600g. They have exceptionally long fingers for probing into bark for invertebrates, and have very distinctive manes. The three species of this tamarin, Golden Headed lion,

MARMOSET HAND
SHOWING CLAWS

MARMOSET FOOT
SHOWING CLAWS

Golden Rump lion and the Golden lion, are the most endangered in the wild.

There are twelve races of callitrichids listed as rare, vulnerable or indeterminate by the International Union of Conservation of Nature and Natural Resources (IUCN), in the mammal red data book. Most are affected by habitat loss, and capture for the pet trade and research, and in the past zoos have similarly affected some species, such as the Cotton-topped tamarin.

The name marmoset comes from the French *marmoute*, which translated means 'grotesque figure' or 'young monkey'. The generic name for tamarins, 'saguinus', derives from the French for 'squirrel monkey'.

They live in bisexual groups, which include a dominant pair, single breeding female and two or more sets of offspring. Sub-adult Tamarins sometimes form breeding groups within the dominant pair's territory. Marmoset groups are more stable.

The most common and prolonged social behaviour is that of grooming between breeding adults, and their most recent offspring. This helps to establish group social relationships. Territorial defence includes display of genitals and stiff legged walking, with arched back, by dominant males. All species call at and chase rivals, and some tongue-flick.

All callitrichids have high whistles which can indicate states of fear, anger and danger. Pygmy marmoset trills are used mainly for communication.

Common marmoset noise is normally an excitement pattern. Golden-lion trills, whines, clucks and chattering are used during solo activities.

Marmosets and tamarins have the least specialised feet and hands of all primates. All digits are clawed except the big toe, which has a broad flat nail. These claws enable the animals to cling to tree trunks and branches, and are used as tools for foraging for insects and impaling them, and tearing at bark on trees.

Tree exudates (gums and saps) are particularly important features of many wild marmoset diets. As a result, marmosets require smaller territories than the more frugivorous (fruit eating) tamarins.

The Pygmy marmoset spends around 80% of its waking hours making hundreds of holes per square metre of tree trunk, to gather the sweet saps and gums, which in turn gives a constant supply of minerals, trace elements and sugar. Other marmosets and tamarins also tap these exudates, but only as a dietary supplement when other foods are not available.

All are omnivorous, feeding on a variety of fruits, buds and small animals. Tamarins are adept at catching lizards and frogs, whereas the Pygmy marmoset catches insects and spiders. Water is obtained by lapping dew or rain, which can collect in tree hollows. Scent marking is a regular occurrence, and this is used for marking routes, sleeping areas, exudate trees, boundaries and mates.

In marmoset groups, only the dominant female breeds. Her partner may mate with other mature females, but it is thought that ovulation may be inhibited by scent wafted from the dominant female's sebaceous glands. These subordinate females remain infertile until all traces of the scent are removed.

Pair bonding is permanent, and family groups vary from two to eight. Under normal conditions, three or four individuals make up the group. Births are seasonal, during September to March in the wild.

The smallest callitrichids are the Pygmy marmosets. Adults weigh around 150g. Their length only attains 29–38cm, which includes the tail. Family groups number from two up to fifteen individuals and usually occupy adjacent overlapping home-ranges.

Callitrichids normally give birth to twins, although it is not uncommon for triplets or singletons to be produced. In contrast, the Goeldis monkey, a primate which taxonomically lies between the marmoset and the tamarin, normally bears a single infant. Common and Pygmy marmosets produce two litters per year, but the Cotton-topped tamarin is seasonal and produces only one litter.

Gestation varies between 128 and 155 days depending on the species. All callitrichid species members carry and care for the offspring. In most species, other marmosets or tamarins are allowed to take infants from the mother within three days of birth.

Sexual maturation is reached within 12–18 months, and physical maturation is at 18–24 months.

Many species of callitrichids are kept in captivity, but the most usual is the Common Marmoset. These can now be bought through some of the larger pet shops and many animal dealers. Caging for such animals has to be strong, since they can, as already highlighted, use their teeth and claws for tearing at timbers. It is therefore important that their enclosures are large enough for sufficient cage furniture to be put in, so as to prevent the main structure from being attacked. A minimum size of 2m high, 1.2m deep and 1.2m wide, is suitable for one pair of marmosets, if kept indoors. Naturally, the larger the cage the better, as when cage furniture and nest boxes are introduced the activity area of the cage is dramatically reduced.

The indoor cage should be constructed on a solid base, avoiding if possible the use of wooden floors, unless covered, because these will encourage dampness from spills and urine that could eventually start to rot and smell, and which in turn may harbour infection. A concrete base is suitable, if it is to be covered with deep litter. I would recommend the use of bark strippings as a deep litter, so that cleaning of the cage can be minimised, although waste food must be taken out daily. This form of litter gives the animals the opportunity to forage, and absorbs most moisture.

The walls of the indoor cage can be made of heavy duty plywood, if a natural wall cannot be used. The wood must not be treated, but it can be painted with a non-toxic paint. As some marmosets gouge wood with their lower incisor teeth, a brick built cage may be built, but this presents a rather cold environment, so the brickwork would need to be overlaid with plastic-covered board or Formica. It also makes cleaning easier if the walls are kept smooth.

The front of the cage can be wired with a suitable mesh, (25mm by 25mm) 16 gauge twilweld being the most suitable. An alternative is to glaze the front, keeping in mind the need for suitable ventilation. The ceiling of the cage should also be made of a rigid material, as this will help to hold the vertical poles of the cage furniture.

The furniture for the minimum sized cage described could be three upright stripped larch poles, about 5cm in diameter, with a number of similar sized poles bolted on to form horizontal runs. Once the main framework has been constructed, twiggy branches can be tied to it to create a more tree-like appearance. The heated nest box can be included inside the cage, with an intermediary slide to enable it to be used as a catch-up facility. The box needs to be made from heavy duty plywood which must be left untreated, but can be painted with a non-toxic paint. The size should be 75cm high, 45cm deep, and 45cm wide, with a hinged door 30cm high. The top 15cm of the box contains the heat lamp, which is separated from the rest by a mesh panel, so that the animals cannot come in direct contact or interfere with it. A 10cm square entrance hole is cut in the door, 7.5cm from the bottom. This gives access to the heated box for the animals, and is sufficiently large to cope with an adult carrying young.

Within the main box is a smaller box, measuring 25cm high, 20cm wide, and 20cm deep. Again, a 10cm square hole is made in the front of the box,

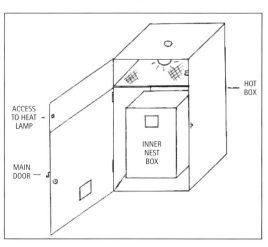

but this time 5cm from the top to allow the animals to go in and down, for privacy. They can use the top of the small box for more direct heat, as it is positioned directly below the heat lamp, which is protected by the mesh. I have found that this type of heated nest box gives the animals the choice of being very warm (24°C, 74°F) on top of the small box, adequately warm (21°C, 70°F), by being inside the small box or in the large box generally, or at the ambient temperature in the fresh air of the main cage.

If an outdoor cage is to be used as the main activity area, it needs to be at least as big as the indoor cage, but preferably larger. It can be constructed of a wooden framework with (25mm by 25mm mesh size) 16 gauge twilweld attached. The floor can be the same as the internal cage, but if a natural earth floor is to be left, then try to ensure that the ground is clean, because infection from rodent and bird droppings can occur. A solution of Jeyes fluid and water can be applied to the soil and will kill most infections (see the instructions on the can for details of dilution rates).

The roof should be part covered, to allow protection from the elements, and from the risk of infection carried by wild birds' droppings. Boarding at the bottom of the sides of the cage will help to prevent rodents from entering and contaminating the floor of the enclosure. Suitable bolts top and bottom are essential on all doors, and where possible a double door should be installed to prevent escapes.

When installing electricity to the heated box, always ensure that the wire is protected or out of reach of the animals, or they may bite through the cables.

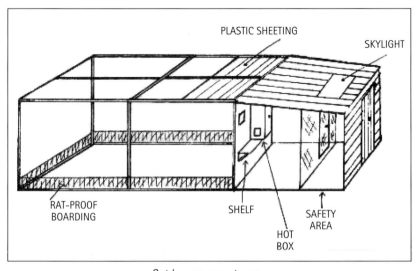

Outdoor marmoset cage

DIET

As already outlined, marmosets and tamarins feed on a variety of foodstuffs in the wild. Most of these foods can be supplied in captivity, although the exudates present a problem. I have always given a sweet mixture which is prepared each day, made from infant cereal food, milk powder and sugar, mixed with warm water, into a creamy consistency. Fresh fruit, vegetables, wholemeal bread and mineral and vitamin supplements are given daily. Live food such as crickets can be given three or four times a week, and mealworms once a week.

A typical daily diet for a pair of marmosets would be:

½ banana
½ apple
½ pear
½ orange (peeled)
½ tomato
½ carrot
2 dried figs
½ slice of wholemeal bread

all the above cut into small cubes and sprinkled with a suitable mineral and vitamin supplement such as SA37.

The daily 'nectar' ration is made as follows:

10g Milupa baby cereal (fruit flavours are preferred by the animals)
2g milk powder
¼ teaspoon sugar.

This is mixed with warm water to form a creamy consistency. The nectar mix can be given first thing in the morning, followed at midday with the main meal. Insects can be given during the day, or, if an insect dispenser is installed, then the animals will cope with that themselves.

Other foods that can be tried are: day old chick legs, pieces of cooked chicken, grapes and other soft fruits available, yoghurt, cream cheese, sunflower seeds, peanuts, tinned dog or cat food, root vegetables cooked and raw, sweet biscuit, and hard boiled egg. Give these in small quantities, to see what your animals prefer, but look upon them as additions to the normal diet.

There are many simulated diets to be obtained, such as marmoset jelly. This is supplied as a white powder, with a powdered flavour that can be added. The powder is mixed with the flavouring and then dissolved in hot water and allowed to cool. It sets as a jelly which can then be cut into cubes or strips and offered to the marmosets. This form of food is high in protein, and high in energy, and gives the animals most of the nutrients they require. It can prove to be an expensive method of feeding, though, and some marmosets do not take to it readily.

Marmosets and tamarins require a high input of vitamin D3 in their diet and, as said previously, they do not obtain it in their normal daily captive rations. A concentrate D3 powder is now available through your veterinary surgeon, and this is administered on the dry food after mixing it into glucose powder at a rate of 1g D3 to 500g glucose; be sure to mix them well together. This mixture is dusted over the food daily, and should give an adequate level of vitamin D3 to prevent any bone deformities occurring.

Other additives that can be given to these primates, to increase their vitamin intake, are Cytacon B12 and ABIDEC, which are available from most chemists. A few drops weekly in the 'nectar' mix should be sufficient.

Water must be given daily, and all feeding utensils must be emptied, washed thoroughly, and dried each day before fresh food is put into them. Plastic 'D' cups can be used as food containers, but these eventually get scratched and can harbour germs. Stainless steel bowls are more suitable, and can be obtained from most good pet stores. A hooked ring fits onto the wire of the cage, and a round stainless steel bowl drops into the ring. Having no corners to trap food makes them easy to clean. Always make sure that the animals have easy access to the feed bowls, by having a horizontal perch about 5cm away.

BREEDING

Obtaining your first pair of animals can be a very exciting experience, but it is important to make sure that they come from different blood lines. If they happen to be related, then breeding them may bring forth offspring which are unhealthy, runted or deformed.

Sexing of marmosets and tamarins can prove to be difficult, but the obvious method is to examine the genitalia.

Common marmosets normally breed quite readily, if the conditions are correct, from about 18 months of age, and may produce two litters per year.

Oestrus cycles in the female vary between 14 and 24 days. Most species have a postpartum oestrus, 2–10 days after giving birth, at which conception can take place.

The gestation period for the Common marmoset is usually 140–149 days. Most litters are born in either in the spring or late summer, but they can breed during most months of the year.

Births normally take place at night, or in the early hours of the morning.

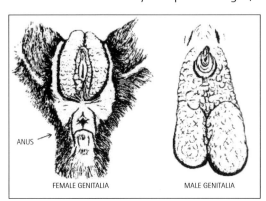

ANUS

FEMALE GENITALIA   MALE GENITALIA

Marmoset genitalia

Observation of births shows that the male stands behind the female and, once the baby has arrived, helps to clear and eat the afterbirth and places the baby on his back. When the second baby arrives, the same procedure is followed. The male then carries the youngsters for the first few days, only passing them to the female for feeding. After this period, both adults take turns in carrying the young.

Twins are normal, but triplets can occur. Triplets can present a problem, since the female has only two nipples. She will normally feed both youngsters at the same time, so a third youngster may be neglected and die. It is possible, though, to remove the youngster for hand-rearing. This is a very time-consuming process, as for the first week the infant will have to be fed on a 1–2 hourly basis. Much good hand-rearing has been done in the past, and one of the most successful people in this field is Lady Fisher, who used to own and run the Kilverstone Wildlife Park in Thetford, Norfolk, which unfortunately is now closed. Her successes exceed one hundred individual animals.

Methods of hand-rearing differ between marmoset owners, but, during my experiences, I have adopted a method similar to Lady Fisher's and have had good results. This is the method that is described here.

To ensure that the infant is being kept at the right temperature, a plant propagator (set at about 25–28°C, 76°–82°F) is an ideal incubator/nursery. A woolly jumper or soft towelling should be put into the propagator, and something for the youngster to cling to, such as a small soft toy, will help to give it some form of security.

The smallest 'Catac' feeding bottle, available from most pet stores, is used with a ST1 teat. To regulate the flow of milk, a teat without a hole in it from a human baby bottle is obtained and is placed on the end of the 'Catac' bottle. With a little pressure on this teat, it is possible to regulate the amount of milk leaving the bottle and entering the baby marmoset's mouth.

From my experiences with hand-rearing, the first five days are the most crucial. Although two-hourly feeds are given, I have always offered extra food every hour, sometimes in the form of a glucose feed. The animal may

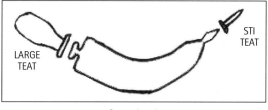

Catac bottle

not take each additional feed, but this is the period when the internal organs need to receive as much nutrition as possible, for proper growth. A young marmoset which was being reared by its parents died at five days old, and at post-mortem was found to have underdeveloped internal organs. This was attributed to the mother having insufficient nutrients in her milk.

It is also important to remember that, after each feed, the abdomen of the youngster should be carefully wiped with a moist tissue, to induce defecation.

A typical hand-rearing procedure for the first five weeks of life follows:

- Between day 1 and day 5, SMA (human baby milk powder obtainable from chemists), is given at each two-hourly feed. The dilution is one scoop added to 28ml of boiled water, administered at body temperature with a 'Catac' bottle. The youngster will normally take around 0.5ml. Into one feed daily, put one drop of ABIDEC.

- Between two-hourly feeds, give a glucose feed: one teaspoon of glucose powder to 28ml of boiled water. Around 0.5ml will be taken by the youngster, at body heat. The remainder can be kept in the 'fridge, but always remember to warm the liquid to body heat before giving it to the youngster.
- Between days 6 and 14, continue with the SMA and ABIDEC as above, but also add a little Milupa infant cereal (fruit flavour). Mix the Milupa to a paste, and add to the milk. This is now giving extra bulk to the animal, and will help in providing some of the trace elements that it requires.
- Between weeks 2 and 3, start to introduce vitamin D3 twice a week. This comes in powder form, and can be mixed with arachis oil, which makes it easier to administer. The youngster will require 1000iu per week, to ensure that bone deformities do not occur.
- By week 4, the feeds should be around every three hours, and the SMA reduced and the Milupa increased. In addition, the youngster may now be offered a little mashed banana to introduce it to solid food. This will be a trial-and-error period, but do not try to force the animal to eat: it will do so in its own time.
- By week 5, the youngster should now be taking some solid food, and other fruits can be added to the diet. Use mainly soft fruits, and allow the animal to try a piece of carrot to chew.

The following weeks will show a sharp increase in its diet, and several other foods can be introduced (see section on feeding).

Bottle feeds should be continued as long as possible, to give a certain amount of security to the youngster, but these can be reduced as it more readily takes to feeding itself from a bowl.

At about nine weeks old, the youngster can be reintroduced to the parents. Rejection by the parents can occur, but if they are 'teased' with the youngster, they will usually snatch it from the hand, and their protective instincts then take over.

Youngsters are left with their parents for at least 15 months, before being taken away. This is to ensure that they have learnt from the parents how to care for offspring, and other normal behaviour patterns.

Inexperienced youngsters, that have been taken away from their parents before this age, usually destroy their first litter, and possibly some later litters.

As with most animals, inadequate diet and bad housing can create disease and imperfections, but, with a good variety of foodstuffs and reasonably heated housing, they should stay in perfect health.

Draughts and dampness can be fatal to marmosets and tamarins, and they are very prone to human ailments such as colds and herpes, as well as other respiratory viruses. So take care to avoid passing these on to them.

DISEASES

Common Cold
A simple human common cold can be a disaster to a marmoset or tamarin. Pneumonia can soon develop and can prove to be fatal.

Dental Problems
Abscesses are not uncommon, and are usually associated with the canine teeth.

Caries
This is a condition in which teeth decay and eventually disintegrate, in animals that are fed on man-made sugary foods.

Diarrhoea
Loose stools (droppings) can be passed by frightened animals as a result of stress, or from too much fruit in the diet. Stools which are very fluid should be examined by a veterinary surgeon. If the animal continues to pass them, it will lose weight, and if untreated eventually die.

Escherichia Coli
This is a bacterial infection which can prove fatal to marmosets and tamarins. I have found that yearly vaccinations with 'Porcovac' have helped to eliminate the problem. Your vet should be able to help with obtaining and administering this vaccine.

Hepatitis
This virus can easily be transmitted from many species of monkey including marmosets and tamarins, to humans.

Herpes Virus Infections

These include the common cold sore, which can be transmitted to the animals from humans, and may be fatal. Herpes virus B can be transmitted from marmosets and tamarins to humans by a bite or scratch, and may cause serious illness. Most herpes viruses cause lesions on the lips, palate, cheeks and gums of the animal. Any animal suspected of being infected should be isolated from any others using a net or gloves, and a veterinary surgeon called. The isolated animal should be kept warm at 24°C (76°F).

Measles

This can be transmitted from human children and adults, and may be fatal to the animal. Signs to look for are a rash, loss of weight, diarrhoea and discharge from the nostrils.

Mumps

This can be contracted from humans, but affects young animals more than adults.

Pneumonia

This can be passed on to the animals from humans and the usual symptoms are loss of appetite, loss of condition, respiratory distress, and if left untreated can result in death.

Tuberculosis

This disease causes emaciation and, if the lungs are involved, respiratory distress. Although the majority of infections arise within the group of monkeys, it can also be contracted from man.

All of the above problems have the potential to be very serious and some are communicable to humans, so strict rules of hygiene should be followed with any sick animal, and the vet called quickly.

11

FISH (Pisces)

Fish, like reptiles, are cold-blooded, which means their bodies are at the same temperature as the surrounding environment. They take in oxygen by gulping water through the mouth, which enters the gill chamber when the mouth closes. Then oxygen and

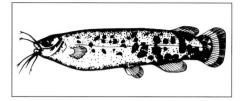

Catfish

carbon dioxide are exchanged, the same as in land animals' lungs. Once this process is completed, the water is discharged through the gills.

Fins help a fish to swim, and also allow it to balance, that is to keep it upright, and to move in the water. The side fins and the underneath fins at the front control up-and-down and side-to-side movements. The fins on the top of the fish and the rear bottom fins control movement both backwards and forwards. The tail fin provides the power of propulsion.

Most fish have scales, which are small disc-like outer coverings that overlap each other, very much like tiling on a house. A layer of secreted mucus covers the scales to aid the fish to slide through the water easily, and also helps protect against disease. This whole outer skin is waterproof.

Many fish have a dark coloration on the top of their bodies and light coloration underneath. This helps the fish from being preyed upon by other animals. From above the water, the top of the fish blends in with the dark floor of the waterbed. From below, the light underneath blends in with the sunlit water on the surface.

Fish have reasonably good eyesight, although there are some species which are blind. Some can detect movement in the water from some 17m away. Sighted fish have two eyes, one on either side of the head, but they do not possess eyelids.

They have inner ears which are within the cranium, and sounds are received by vibrations from body tissue. Similar to many other animals, fish depend on their sense of smell to find food and habitat, and the nostrils are located on the head.

Although a fish's taste buds are located on the mouth and the tongue, they are also present on the head and the body.

Along each side of a fish's body is a series of tiny openings in a line, which are sensitive to vibrations in the water. This helps the fish's balance and also its depth observation. This is called the lateral line.

Some other fish have further means of employing the sense of touch, such as barbels and electric receptors.

The body design of some fish is torpedo-shaped, which allows them to move through the water with more swiftness than any other body shape. Other fish have different body shapes, and other protective devices to help in their survival e.g. camouflage, venom, armour, spines and electricity.

CARTILAGINOUS FISH

These fish have a skeleton, including the skull and jaws, which consists entirely of cartilage, and no bony tissue is present. An example

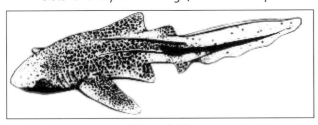

Nurse shark

of this is the shark. There are some 600 species of cartilaginous fish, the shark being the oldest known. Deposits containing their teeth and spines have been found which date back over 400 million years.

The normal swim-bladder is absent in these fish, so they have to swim constantly, or sink to the bottom.

Some species are egg layers, ovoviviparous, and produce their eggs in horny capsules with either coiled tendrils at the corners, as with the sharks, or with pointed horns as with the rays. These are generally known as 'mermaids' purses'. Other species are live bearers, viviparous, the young hatching and developing within the female.

Spines are present in some species, and these are in front of the two dorsal fins, e.g. Spur Dog shark, or at the base of the tail, e.g. stingrays. These spines can inject venom.

The largest of all fish, reaching 13–15 metres in length, is the Whale Shark, with the Basking Shark a close second at 11–12 metres.

BONY FISH

These are the majority of fish living today: there are some 25,000 species known. All species of this group have some bone within the skeleton. Most species are oviparous, egg layers, sometimes producing many thousands of eggs, with embryos developing outside the mother's body.

Rainbow trout

This is unlike ovoviviparous fish, which bear young developed from eggs retained within the mother's body, but separated from it by the egg membranes.

Some species of bony fish are viviparous, bearing live young that have developed in the mother's body, which are nourished by the placenta, which also takes away waste products.

Teeth vary in the bony fish, naturally depending on the individual feeding habits. Predatory fish have large pointed teeth like fangs, whereas fish that feed on shellfish have flat crushing teeth.

The largest bony fish is the Arspaima of South America, which attains a length of 5 metres, and the smallest is the Goby from the Philippines, which does not grow any longer than 12.5mm.

The feeding habits of fish vary greatly, and I have set out some examples below just for interest:

Carp – feed on tiny plants and animals obtained by rooting on the bottom of rivers and streams.

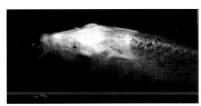

Carp

Catfish – feed on live and dead food found on the bottom of lakes and ponds, but can also side feed, which is more obvious if observed in an aquarium.

Electric Eel – uses its electrical discharge to stun other fish and then devour them. The long tail contains specialised muscles which make up the 'electric organs', capable of discharging up to 600 volts.

Piranha – a purely carnivorous fish that can devour a large animal in seconds. When hungry they bite anything which moves, and normally hunt in shoals.

Arawana – this fish is found living in fresh streams in South America, Africa, SE Asia and north Australia. Because of its long lower jaw and mouth position, it is a surface feeder.

Bass – the smaller species of bass feed on shrimps and crustaceans, but the larger species feed on fish, such as sand eels, sprat, herring and pilchard.

Haddock – feeds off molluscs, sea urchins, and small fish. A similar fish to the Cod, but has a black spot above the pectoral fin and no spots on the flanks.

Herring – one of the best known of the bony fish, lives off plankton, minute aquatic organisms that drift with the water movements and have no locomotive organs.

Tope – a member of the shark family found around British waters, feeds off mackerel on the surface and crabs on the bottom.

Dogfish – another of the shark family also found around the British shores, feeds chiefly on worms, whelks, crustaceans, young cuttlefish and sea urchins.

Mullet – usually grub about on the bottom, filtering out minute animals and plants by using their gill-rakers.

From these examples, you can see that different fish feed at different levels within the water habitat, using specialist techniques to do so. In tropical oceans, flying fish can be observed actually jumping and gliding through the air. We generally see fish swim, but some glide, crawl, climb, leap, hop, burrow, and some move by jet propulsion. This demonstrates that fish have adapted themselves fully to marine life.

If we look carefully at a marine community, we find that there are more layers of consumers than in a land-based community. An invertebrate food-chain of bottom dwellers, and a food pyramid of vertebrates and inverte-brates which inhabit open waters, can be described as follows:

The lowest but the largest layer of the pyramid is made of the phyto-plankton (minute plant life). Next comes the plankton (minute animal forms) which feed off the phytoplankton. Then come the small fish feeding on the plankton. Next, the fewer larger fish feeding off the smaller fish, then the largest fish feeding off them. If we look at it as a model of producers and consumers, then the phytoplankton is the producer and the rest are the consumers.

Fish- keeping has become a widespread hobby, with specialist shops, many magazines and books available, and experienced amateur aquarists who know a great deal about their animals. I shall outline the basic requirements for setting up various tanks, to give beginners some idea of what they are letting themselves in for.

The most common fish to obtain at the lowest price are goldfish (Carassius auratus), although many small fresh-water and even salt-water species are suitable for home aquaria. These animals are reasonably easy to look after. They require very little space, are not costly to maintain, are odourless and noiseless, and fun to watch. In fact aquaria seem to have a relaxing effect on humans. Fish are mostly diurnal, (active during the daytime), and can be observed at all times in a glass aquarium, where they will thrive and possibly breed.

In addition to goldfish, popular fresh water species include guppies from the Caribbean, fighting fish from Thailand, swordtails from Mexico and Central America etc.

The salt water species of fish are a bit more diffi-cult to obtain and maintain, although the amount of

Yellow tang

literature available on this subject is becoming more abundant. Species include the neon goby from the tropical Atlantic and Caribbean, the damselfish from the Caribbean and the Pacific, groupers and other sea bass from the Indo-Pacific and many others.

Native fish may be kept in aquaria, as can a host of other animals such as snails, insects such as water-boatmen, as well as various plants.

Never use a fish bowl to keep your animals in, as the water surface is too small to take in sufficient oxygen. Use a good quality glass tank which is made with either a stainless steel or a heavy plastic frame, depending on the size, made watertight with a thin layer of aquarium cement, which allows for changes in water pressure and temperature. These start at about £20 ($29) for a small tank with lid, and go up to over £100 ($145) for the larger, more ornate aquaria. Additional to this will be lighting, filter unit and, if required, a heater. This could set you back a further £50–100, or more for larger aquaria.

Once the exhibit is set up, never try to lift the tank whilst it is full of water. You probably will not be able to do it, as for example a 90 litre (20 gallon) capacity aquarium will weigh over 90kgs, but more importantly it would be very dangerous, not only to you but to the animals inside.

A cover is required to keep the fishes in and foreign matter out, and most modern aquaria come already fitted with one. Try not to buy a second-hand tank for your first exhibit of fish. If the tank is old, cracks may have formed in the cement, allowing the water to seep through.

The size of the tank will vary according to the species and number of fish to be kept. A good guide for size is that for every 25mm of fish, 5 litres of water is required, although some experienced aquarists prefer a ratio of surface area to fish size. If keeping marine species, then a minimum of 100 litres capacity should be the size of your aquarium.

All aquaria should be kept out of direct sunlight if algae are to be prevented from taking over, and should be artificially lit from the top so the fish can be given at least 12 hours of light per day. Temperature can vary between 24°C (75°F) and 26°C (78°F) for fresh water fish and even higher for some species, but may be cooler for salt water species. A thermometer is an essential piece of equipment, as is a filter which will ensure that the water is always aerated with oxygen and that some of the impurities are taken from it. The water that is put into the aquarium originally should be specially conditioned or aged before fish can live in it, in order to take out any toxic elements. Tap water may be conditioned by standing exposed in shallow non-metal containers, or by having compressed air forced through it, or by introducing aquatic plants.

In marine aquaria, filtration is especially important to prevent harmful substances, such as ammonia and organic matter from uneaten food, faeces, or dead fish, from building up.

Bacteria on the gravel will form a natural biological filtration, and gravel itself will help to sift out certain substances. Activated carbon will get rid of the rest chemically and is recommended for all marine tanks.

Plants do not guarantee a perfect ecological cycle or balance, since they make carbon dioxide at night, which may be fatal to fish if over-produced. Plants do provide suitable sites for the attachment of eggs, create places for some less aggressive fish to hide, and make tanks more natural-looking.

Sea water can be collected from the shore, and, because minerals do not evaporate with the water, the addition of aged water will keep the mineral concentration at the appropriate levels. Always let new sea water stand for at least three weeks in a dark room, to stabilise it before use. Siphon out any silt, and aerate the water for about 12 hours before you add any fish. Synthetic sea water is available and requires less preparation.

When setting up your tank, try to use commercial aquarium sand or gravel. Your aquarist shop will supply you with all your needs, and the advice you may need from time to time.

There are many suitable plants for both fresh water and marine tanks, but it is best to ask your aquarist's advice on the types to use for your tank. Some have roots, others do not and float. Too many plants can be harmful to your fish.

When the water in your aquarium turns green, there is too much algae in it, which some aquarists believe is good for the fish as it protects them from the light, but it may actually be dangerous, especially on hot days. The problem can be solved by starving the plant life in the tank by feeding the fish live food or less food, or by aerating the water, or by introducing a few litres of new water.

Put in your plants at least a couple of days before you introduce your fish to the tank. It is advisable to start with inexpensive fish, adding only a few at a time, until you are sure that the aquarium is functioning properly.

Once it is functioning, then other animals such as leeches, snails, and water insects can be introduced which help to clean up after the fish, but they may also take fish eggs. A marine aquarium can also support such creatures as tiny crabs, starfish, sea anemones etc.

The feeding of fish has been simplified over the years, with more and more prepared foods available. Prepared dried foods contain beef liver, cereal, and vegetable matter such as lettuce and spinach, and are the least expensive. In addition to this food, which is available from all aquarists, live food such as daphnia, white worms, and rubiform worms, can be given on occasions, say once or twice a week depending on the species. This too can be bought from your local aquarist.

It is advisable to feed daily, giving small quantities at a time. If any food is left after five minutes, reduce the next feed accordingly. All food left in the tank will eventually rot and sour and cloud the water, as well as stimulate the growth of plants to a dangerous level. It has been said that overfeeding fish is responsible for more aquarium failures than any other error.

12

GENERAL REFERENCE SECTION

BOA CONSTRICTOR (Boa constrictor constrictor)

Distribution: Central and South America
Cost: £50 ($72) up to £200 ($290) depending on size
of animal
Availability: from most large pet shops or dealers
Things to look for: make sure the animal is not
shedding its skin when you buy it. If the scaling of the snake looks milky,
then possibly it is about to shed. This is a bad time to touch one, since for
a short period it cannot see so well, because the old eye spectacle is lifting
from the new spectacle (it is attached to the surrounding skin). In addition
the rest of the snake's skin is becoming loose and can be an irritant, which
in turn can make it aggressive. No good pet shop or dealer will sell an
animal in this condition.

Check for ticks under the scales, especially if the boa is newly imported.
If they are there, then get them removed before you buy it, especially if
you want to introduce it to an already existing one, as ticks can be
transferred to other snakes.
Longevity: as with most of the large constrictors, Boas can live 20 years
or more.
Size: when born, they are about 30–38cm in length. At about six months
they will attain a length of some 75cm, and at one year old about 115cms.
This naturally depends on the way the animal has been kept, how it has
been fed, and whether it was wild-caught or captive-bred. They grow
eventually to around 5–6m.
Sexual maturity: 3–4 years old.

Breeding: these snakes give birth to live young: anything from 10 to 60 can be born at any one time.

Caging cost: around £100 ($145) for a large purpose-built vivarium, but to run heating and lighting will cost a further £50 ($73) per annum. Feeding is about £2 ($3) per feed plus additives cost. See also the chapter on reptiles.

Captive diet: when young, give small rodents. Larger snakes will take large rats, rabbits, chickens.

Diseases: see chapter on reptiles.

Comments: these snakes are not so easy to come by, and the prices are escalating. Buying a large snake could present problems, especially if you are not used to them, and, if they have not been handled much, they can tend to be a little snappy. My advice is to buy a young one, and handle it as much as you possibly can, to give you and it the confidence needed.

BURMESE PYTHON (Python molurus bivittatus)

Distribution: India, southern China

Cost: from £50 ($73) for a youngster up to over £200 ($290) for a large adult

Availability: more available than the Boa

Longevity: can live up to 35 years

Size: when born they are 30–37cm, but they can attain a length of over 5m when fully adult

Sexual maturity: 4–5 years of age

Breeding: unlike the boas, pythons lay eggs. A normal clutch can be up to 40 eggs, of which 25–30 will hatch. This has been my experience when breeding this species but in the wild up to 100 eggs may be laid. They are normally laid in late spring, with a gestation period of 60–80 days, depending on the temperature of the vivarium.

Caging: as for the boas

Diet: as for the boas

Diseases: see chapter under reptiles

Comments: this snake is one of the easiest to handle, and I have never known anyone get bitten, except those who handle them badly, or when the snake is sloughing its skin, or from silly things, like trying to pick the animal up after handling another animal such as a rat.

The Burmese python is very similar to the Indian python but is not so rare. The Indian python has reduced in numbers, mainly because of the trapping of them for their fine skins. The grey-coloured specimens found mainly in western parts of India are used by the 'snake charmers' because the animals are not so aggressive as their cousins.

These animals hunt by night, searching for any small or large mammals, and on occasions take birds as well. Like all constrictors they grasp their prey with their fangs and then instantly coil around the victim, suffocating it. Once the animal ceases to move it is swallowed whole, head first.

During the day they bask in the heat of the sun or rest in crevices and caves.

CHINCHILLA (Chinchilla laniger)

Distribution: South America.
Cost: a single animal will cost £40-65 ($58-95).
Availability: obtainable from breeders and large pet shops.
Longevity: in captivity they can live between 6 and 10 years.
Size: a little larger in body size than a guinea pig when fully grown, although it weighs less.
Sexual maturity: 9-12 months old.
Breeding: average of two young after 110 days gestation. They normally breed in December and March.
Caging: will cost £20-30 ($29-43) for a suitable hutch. The best way to keep these animals is to allow them to climb, therefore a tall cage with a nesting box is desirable. See chapter on rodents.
Diet: standard chinchilla pellets and a little root vegetable and apple. Cost of feeding around £1-2 per week depending on the number of animals kept.
Diseases: see chapter on rodents.
Comments: these lovely animals need a lot of care, but not too much handling, as their fur is very fine and does tend to come away very easily, especially if touched with moist hands. Chinchillas live in large colonies in the wild: anything up to 100 specimens may be found sheltering in many holes and crevices in the rocks. The females are generally larger than the males and also become aggressive to one another.

Chinchillas feed on lichen and any other vegetation that is available at the time. When eating they sit bolt upright with the tail to balance, and hold their food in their front paws. The rarity of these animals in the wild is due to their being captured for their fine, soft, dense coats for the fur trade, although nowadays they are farm bred almost all over the world. See main chapter on rodents.

GECKO (Many species available)

Distribution: Australia, East Indies, India, South-east Asia.
Cost: from £15 ($22) upwards.
Availability: can be obtained from large specialist pet shops and dealers.
Longevity: depending on the species, 10 years or more.
Size: adults grow to 30cm.
Sexual maturity: 2–3 months old.
Breeding: very difficult in captivity.
Caging: a wooden or glass vivarium, heated to a temperature of 24–30°C (74°–86°F). The vivarium should be a minimum of 1m long, 30cm deep, and 40cm high or higher. A good, well ventilated, secure lid should be fitted, and plenty of branches for climbing put inside. Sand should cover the floor, with pieces of bark and rocks where the animals can hide. A small container for water should also be included. These are a nocturnal species so will not normally be active during the day. Cost of vivarium will be between £20 ($29) and £30 ($43) but heating and lighting will be a further £50 ($73) per year, plus replacement bulbs.
Diet: small live insects such as housefly, fruitfly, mealworms, termites. *Feeding is minimal*: about £1–2 per week.
Diseases: the most common ailment with this species is limb deformity, usually caused by a calcium deficiency. Add standard reptile additives to the diet.

If the animal has a good appetite but is losing weight, this could indicate that it has an internal parasite. Veterinary advice should be sought.

If it has a discharge from the nostrils, this could be a form of bacterial pneumonia. Veterinary advice should be sought.
Comments: there are probably up to 700 species of gecko, all living in the tropical and subtropical areas of the world. They occupy all habitats

that have a sufficient amount of insect life to feed on, and where the temperature is more or less constant, especially at night. Deserts, forests, water courses and mountains are generally the areas for these animals to be found. A gecko has a flat head, large eyes, and a body covered in soft skin containing many tiny scales. Handling can be difficult as their tails tend to break off, and their skin tears very easily. They can also bite.

Being a nocturnal animal, they are not as interesting to observe as others of the lizard family.

IGUANA (Iguana iguana)

Distribution: South American tropical forests.
Cost: £75 ($110) upwards depending on size.
Availability: usually from larger pet shops or dealers.
Longevity: up to 25 years.
Size: adults can grow to around 1.8m, but they are usually obtainable at about 1m maximum.
Sexual maturity: 2–3 years of age.

Rhinoceros iguana

Breeding: iguanas can lay anything between 6 and 40 eggs but the average is 30. They take 6 weeks to incubate.
Caging: a very large vivarium at least 1.5m long, 1m deep, and 1m high, with a suitable well ventilated, secure lid. This will depend on the size of the animal. The sizes given will be suitable for one of about 1m in length, but remember, it may outgrow this.

It should be heated to 25°–31°C (76°–88°F) and should also have an area for 'sunning'. This can be a large flat rock, suitably placed under a spot light or heat lamp, but make sure the animal cannot touch the lamp. The rest of the cage should have branches to climb, and the floor should be covered with a coarse gravel or paper, or left as bare wood. A reasonably large water dish should also be installed and secured. The cost will be £40–50 ($58–73) for the vivarium and a further £50–75 ($73–110) per year for heating and lighting, plus the cost of replacement bulbs.
Diet: fruit such as banana, apple, pear, grapes, chopped cabbage and carrot, dried dog food, mealworms, boiled egg, raw egg. Give little amounts to see what your animal prefers and give mineral and vitamin additives daily. These can be obtained from any good pet shop. Feeding will cost in the

region of £3 ($4.5) per week depending on the time of the year and the availability of fruits.

Diseases: see under Gecko.

Comments: these animals can get very large, and also have sharp claws and teeth, and can draw blood. If handling one, treat it with respect especially if it is already large when first bought. You don't know if you have taken on someone else's problem! On the other hand they are clean animals, and will enjoy a run round your house (keep the doors shut!).

Llama

LLAMA (Lama glama glama)

Distribution: South America such as Peru and Argentina.
Cost: £350 ($500) upwards per animal.
Availability: these can be obtained through animal dealers and llama breeders. They will not be sold unless suitable housing and grounds are available. In some areas, licensing may be required, or planning. Best to check first.
Longevity: 20–25 years.

Size: these animals will grow to between 100kgs and 240kgs.

Sexual maturity: 2–3 years old.

Breeding: usually between spring and early autumn, having 1 or, on occasion, 2 youngsters. Gestation period is 11 months.

Caging: suitable pasture land or field, approximately 0.25 hectares (half an acre) with a covered internal building of a minimum of 3m square, with plenty of bedding material such as hay or straw.

Diet: A suitable pelleted sheep diet, obtainable from farm suppliers, plus some root vegetables, and hay.

Comments: These animals are relatives of the camel family and are about as easy to look after as sheep, but they do tend to spit when annoyed (and sometimes when not annoyed). The llama, like the alpaca, is the domesticated form of the guanaco and has been bred as an animal of burden, so needs a lot of exercise.

Llamas are ruminants, in which the stomach has three chambers. Food is taken in and after some time the partially digested matter, the cud, is assembled into pellets in the second chamber, the reticulum, ready for regurgitation. This is then chewed thoroughly before passing to the third chamber, where water is absorbed and where normal digestion takes place. The earlier form of llama had hoofs on each foot but through time these have evolved into wide pads on each of the two digits of each foot. When walking they sway from side to side, as the front and back legs on each side move together. They are good wool producers and there are many llama enthusiasts all over the world owning such animals for their wool. A garment made from this wool can be very expensive.

Many books have been written on llamas and these can be found in any library or good bookshop.

LYNX Northern (Felis lynx) and Canadian (Felis lynx canadensis)

Distribution: Germany, Scandinavia, Northern Caucasus, Iraq, Sardinia, Russia, Canada, and as far down as New York State. Also parts of Colorado and the Sierra Nevada; also places in the Midwest of America and Northern California. The American/Canadian species (Felix lynx canadensis) live mostly in mountainous forests, in the more temperate areas.

Cost: from £300 each depending on age of animal.

Availability: not available to individuals unless licencing can be obtained, which is very unlikely. Zoos, wildlife parks etc., can obtain them but they too must obey stringent licencing laws.

Longevity: average is 24 years.

Size: head to tail length is 90–155cm. They stand approximately 70cm high.

Sexual maturity: the males are sexually mature at 3 years old and the females at 2 years old.

Breeding: the lynx breeds between February and March and has a gestation period of just over 2 months. They can produce up to 5 young at a time. The female usually gives birth in a secluded place such as a cave, under the base of trees or even in a disused badger set. As with some other species of cat the male takes no part in the raising of the young.

The young are born furred but blind for up to the first fortnight and suckle from the mother for up to 5 months, although they will start to take solids after 1 month. At this time the young start to move around and even leave the nest. It is documented that youngsters leave when their mothers are due to be mated the following year.

Caging: with all wild cats the caging has to be very strong, usually made of angled steel with wire mesh either welded or bolted onto it. The size of the cage should be as large as is possible bearing in mind the size of the animal. The minimum size would be 10m by 5m and seeing that these creatures can and will climb, a secure roof should complete the structure. The interior of the enclosure should be natural with grass and trees as well as stone ledges where the animals can sunbathe or just rest. A cave-like structure can also be introduced for the animals to use as a breeding area and sleeping den. Adjoining the cage should be inside quarters which they can also sleep in and use for breeding. This area should be a minimum of 3m square and have a central drainage system, for easy cleaning.

Diet: the lynx is an expert hunter and usually hunts alone. Its diet is very varied, ranging from mice to large deer, along with many different birds. In North America the animal is very dependent on local hares in its diet, so much so that the number of animals fluctuates if the hare population decreases.

Diseases: the most common infectious disease nowadays is feline infectious peritonitis (FIP). Adult cats in the wild are not so susceptible to this disease as they have little contact with each other. In captivity the animals are more prone, especially where more than one is kept. The disease attacks the white blood cells throughout the animal's body, and is the biggest form of cat killer there is. The only way to prevent this attacking your animals is to have them vaccinated against it. Most vets will use a one shot combination vaccine which will cover a variety of diseases to include feline 'flu and feline enteritis. Thereafter a yearly booster is given which also gives the opportunity for the vet to give the animals an examination.

Comments: the species from some parts of the Old World such as central and southern Europe are generally spotted, whereas those species in the New World are generally plain grey or light brown. The most distinguishing feature of this cat is the large black-backed pointed ears with long fur tufts. The paws are also covered with a long fur protecting the pads from the cold conditions it lives in. This gives the impression that the animal is wearing boots.

It is documented that the lynx in the Old World is holding its own although it is not so common in Europe. Around twenty years ago some animals were introduced into the southern parts of France, and it is reported that they have successfully established themselves and are breeding well. Trapping for the fur market is prevalent in Asia, but in the wilds of America it is a fairly common animal to be seen. None of the nine subspecies as defined in the International Species Inventory System (ISIS) is endangered. However, many Americans would discourage taking such animals from their natural habitat. It is also the general opinion in Britain, that big cats are ill suited to captivity, and moreover they are covered by the Dangerous Wild Animals Act.

In fact, when this act was passed, some people who owned panthers and lynxes released them into the wild, where they may be breeding.

MACAW (Ara ararauna) Blue and Gold Macaw

Distribution: central and northern parts of South America.
Cost: from £650 ($950) per bird.
Availability: usually available from the larger pet shops and animal dealers.
Longevity: can live up to 50 years of age. Have been known to outlive owners!
Size: average just under 1m in length.
Sexual maturity: 1 year old.
Breeding: from 2 to 4 eggs: incubate for 24 to 26 days.
Caging: see chapter under parrots. If to be kept as a single bird, a suitable-size cage will cost £65–100 ($95–145).

Blue and gold macaws

Diet: mixed seeds, especially sunflower, brazil nuts, unsalted peanuts, walnuts, apple, pear, orange, cabbage stalks, brown bread, mealworms, cuttlefish bone and grit. Fresh water must be available at all times. Feeding will cost in the region of £3–4 per week, per bird.
Diseases: see chapter on parrots.
Comments: like all parrots these can be very destructive. In captivity they can be very dangerous and aggressive if not handled properly.

They are one of the more costly varieties of parrot, due to their coloration, size and longevity. Some species such as the Scarlet macaw are becoming very rare in the wild due to destruction of its habitat within the rain forests of South America. Also the trade in their eggs and young fledglings for the pet trade is still lucrative in South America, although the authorities are beginning to tighten up on this. Most birds now found in pet shops are aviary-bred and not taken from the wild.

The birds maintain strong pairing bonds throughout their lives, are normally seen in pairs, and family groups of up to 20 birds are normal.

They talk well, if taught from an early age. Think twice before buying, as they can be very noisy birds, and can disrupt neighbourly relations.

Common marmoset

MARMOSET – COMMON
(Callithrix jacchus jacchus)

Distribution: northern parts of South America such as north-east Brazil.

Cost: from £150 ($218) per animal

Availability: not so available as they used to be, but can be purchased from most large pet stores or dealers. The only species of marmoset generally available is the Common marmoset.

Longevity: have been known to live up to 12 years in captivity, but average 10 years.

Size: approximately 45cm including tail.

Sexual maturity: from 18 months.

Breeding: breed during most months of the year, having 1-3 babies, 2 being the norm, with a gestation period of 140-149 days.

Caging: see chapter on marmosets and tamarins. Cost will depend on the number of animals to be housed, and whether indoor or outdoor enclosures are to be built. It will start at around £100 ($145) for housing, depending on how many animals are kept. It is never advisable to keep one on its own, because it will fret.

Heating will cost from £2 per week during the winter, and around £1 per week during the summer.

Diet: Fresh fruit such as apple, pear, banana, tomato, orange, some vegetables like carrot, celery or cucumber, wholemeal bread, day-old chick legs, insects, cooked chicken, yoghurt, cheese, nuts, boiled egg, cat and dog food. Cost £5–8 ($7–11) per week for one pair of marmosets. See chapter on marmosets and tamarins for suggested diet.

Diseases: see chapter on marmosets and tamarins.

Comments: marmosets are more available than tamarins. If tamarins are to be bought, then a licence should be acquired beforehand from your local authority. They are not suitable pets to have with other animals because of the spread of disease, and they are not suitable for young children as they have very sharp claws and teeth. They do not like to be handled, but do need a lot of room for exercise. It is not advisable to let them out into your own living room, as they will urinate and defecate anywhere, and also scent mark with a very strong-smelling oil. In addition they will gnaw at any wood.

MONKEY Capuchin (Cebus albifrons)

Distribution: southern Venezuela

Cost: from £150 ($220) upwards depending on species, sex, and age.

Availability: only available from reputable animal dealers but require licence from local authority.

Longevity: in captivity they can live as much as 25 years.

Size: weight around 3kgs.

Sexual maturity: 2–3 years of age.

Breeding: breed throughout the year, having 1 or 2 youngsters, with a gestation period of 6 months.

Caging: these are very active animals and require a lot of room. Minimum requirements I would suggest for one pair of these monkeys, is an outdoor cage 2m deep, 3m long, and as high as is permissible, bearing in mind planning controls by local councils, with an indoor area 2m deep, 2m long fitted with covered heating to a temperature of 21°–26°C (70°–78°F). A large sleeping box should also be included, 1m long, 1m deep and 1m high, filled with hay or straw, with a half-front to enable easy access for both animals. In both outdoor and indoor enclosures, plenty of climbing equipment is needed, such as natural branches and logs. The walls and the ceilings need to be very strongly erected, as these animals are good escape artists, so heavy-duty interlink fencing would be advisable for the outdoor run, with a brick-built indoor structure. Cost of enclosure will be at least

£200 ($290). Heating will be a further £5 ($7.5) per week during the winter period, reducing to £1–2 per week during the summer.

Diet: standard monkey pellets, sunflower and other seeds, mixed nuts, raw meat, fruits, some vegetables such as cabbage and carrot, mineral and vitamin additives sprinkled on the feed daily. Feed small feeds two or three times daily. Add a milk feed such as baby cereal when females are lactating. Feeding will cost from £8 ($12) per week dependent on the availability of fruits, and the number of monkeys.

Diseases: see chapter on marmosets and tamarins, although it is also advisable to get a tetanus inoculation, and take a TB test annually.

Comments: I would not recommend these animals as pets, as they can be very spiteful and sometimes unapproachable, ready to bite at all times. Normally they will only survive well in groups larger than one pair.

MONKEY Rhesus (Macaca mulatta)

Distribution: northern India and Indochina.

Cost and availability: these monkeys which have long breen bred in captivity are readily available, and the cost varies from around £50 ($58) to £150 ($220) per animal. Most are in the hands of protection societies, so it is probably better to contact one of these. A licence is required to own one: applications should be made to the local council.

Longevity: these monkeys can live up to 20 years, although one I had in my charge lived to the ripe age of 30.

Size: in the range of 10–12kgs; they are about the size of a corgi dog.

Sexual maturity: the males are ready at 6 years of age, and the females at 5 years.

Breeding: they breed throughout the year, having one youngster, after a gestation period of 165 days average.

Caging: as for the capuchin monkey.

Diet: as for the capuchin monkey.

Diseases: see chapter on marmosets, although it is also advisable to give a tetanus inoculation.

Comments: again I would not recommend these monkeys as pets, for the same reasons as for the capuchin monkey. Once they become mature, like most other monkeys they can become uncontrollable, especially as house pets.

MONKEY Common Squirrel (Saimiri sciureus sciureus)

Distribution: northern parts of South America.

Cost and availability: these monkeys were once the 'photographer's model', but, because of the treatment they sustained, the deformities of their limbs which occurred because of no proper diet, no free access to water, and the fact that they had to wear starched coats and waist chains which also damaged their fur, they were eventually put on the Dangerous Wild Animal List for their own protection. Now a licence has to be obtained from the local authority before one of these animals can be kept. If this is available, cost is from £350 ($510) per animal. They can be obtained from the larger dealers.

Longevity: in captivity they can reach 20 years, but the average is around 15 years.

Size: They weigh about 1–1.5kgs.

Sexual maturity: 2–3 years

Breeding: they can breed throughout the year, having one youngster after a gestation period of 6 months.

Caging: see chapter on marmosets and tamarins. Costs, the same as for a marmoset.

Diet: the same as for a capuchin monkey.

Diseases: similar to the marmosets and tamarins, but tetanus inoculations and annual TB tests should be taken as a precaution.

Comments: the squirrel monkey only does well in social groups. If on its own it will mope, and not live to a good age. When frightened, like most monkeys they will bite. Normally they can be 'tamed' to the shoulder, but do not like to be handled.

OWL Eagle (Bubo bubo)

Distribution: Europe, North Africa, Asia.

Cost: Over the years, through over-breeding, these owls have come down in price. They are now available at from £75 ($110) per bird.

Availability: from most of the larger animal dealers, and some of the more specialised pet stores.

Longevity: these birds have been known to live to 35 years of age, although the average is about 25 years.

Size: from head to tail the females measure 0.9m, and the males are a little smaller. As with most owls and other birds of prey, the females are usually the larger of the sexes.

Sexual maturity: around 2 years old.

Breeding: normally lay 2–4 eggs, with around a 60-day incubation period.

Caging: being big birds, they require caging large enough for them to be able to stretch their wings fully and at least have some room to fly. A minimum cage for one pair of birds would be 3m long, 2.5m wide, and 2.5m high. Well sheltered back and sides to the aviary, with suitable roofing for the birds to sit under in inclement weather, are needed. A large nest box made of wood, 1m long, 1m high and 0.6m wide, with a half-front and solid roof should suffice, allowing both birds access at any one time.

Cost of this aviary starts at £150 ($220) although wire varies in price and it is wise to look around for odd rolls.

Diet: feed once a day with any from the following. Dead rats, mice, day-old chicks, rabbits, chickens. If from frozen, make sure they are fully defrosted and warmed before being given. A large bath or pond should be built in the enclosure, as these birds do like to bathe regularly. It will cost from £5 ($7.5) per week to feed two birds.

Comments: these birds are the largest of the owl family, and can breed very easily. The only problem is, once they have bred the youngsters are not so easy to move on. They can make good pets, and can be handled if you start when they are youngsters. But see earlier section on owls for potential problems.

SALAMANDER Tiger (Ambystoma tigrinum)

Distribution: North America.

Cost: the price of these does vary but most good pet shops charge around £15 ($22), depending on size and species.

Availability: from many good pet shops and most aquatic and amphibious dealers.

Longevity: can reach 10–15 years in captivity.

Size: normally grow to an adult size of 20–25cm.

Sexual maturity: 12–15 months

Breeding: they can lay up to 500 eggs in one clutch and incubate these for 14–18 days.

Caging: see chapter on amphibians. Cost will be in the region of £20 ($29); heating and lighting a further £1 per week, if required, plus cost of replacement bulbs.

Diet: live food e.g. crickets, earthworms, white worms, mealworms. Cost £1–2 per week.

Diseases: see chapter on amphibians.

Comments: these creatures are easy to keep, but do not expect them to react to human attachments. They can be kept in a mixed collection with frogs and toads, but this may prevent any breeding from occurring. In addition to this a Tiger salamander can grow up to 25cm or more, so therefore it could be a possible threat to other species in the same environment.

It is the world's largest land-dwelling salamander, having a stout body and a very broad head but small eyes. Its colour can vary, but normally it has yellowish or light olive bars across the body which suggests the origin of its name. It lays its eggs in deep-water ponds, and its larvae can be found in such bodies of water from Long Island, down to Florida, and up to the lowland ponds of the Mississippi. Metamorphosis is complete after a few weeks of larval life, and the adult form then comes out of the water and spends the rest of its life on land.

SNAKE Common Garter (Thamnophis sirtalis)

Distribution: North America.

Cost and availability: from around £30 ($73) from any good pet shop or animal dealers. Reasonably common.

Longevity: in captivity can reach 10 years.

Size: adults range from 45cm up to 1.2m.

Sexual maturity: about 2 years of age.

Breeding: up to 80 eggs can be formed, although the average is 15, and the young are born live.

Caging: see chapter on reptiles. Needs a temperature between 21°–31°C (70°–88°F). Cost of vivarium around £20 ($29). Heating will cost from £1 per week.

Diet: live food e.g. earthworms, white worms, mealworms, pieces of raw fish, pieces of raw meat, small live mice (pinkies), small live fresh water minnows, mineral and vitamin supplement once weekly with added cod liver oil. Cost around £3–4 per week.

Diseases: see chapter on reptile diseases.

Comments: the most widespread snake in North America and one of the most common. It has characteristic stripes on its back and sides and the colours of these can vary. It hunts for small amphibians and small invertebrates during the day, exploring the damp vegetation on the ground. It can withstand very cold weather and can be found in the far north of America. Here it hibernates with others during the really cold months, but in the south it remains active all the year.

They sometimes mate as they emerge from hibernation during the spring. Some 80 young snakes develop within the mother's body, which are fed by a form of placenta and are born fully formed and ready to take their place in the world.

These are easy snakes to keep and maintain, once they are used to being confined. They are very active snakes and excellent escape artists, so ensure that a well fitting but well ventilated lid is put on top of the vivarium.

TOAD Common (Bufo bufo)

Distribution: Europe.

Cost: The price of £5 ($7.5) for captive-bred specimens is not unusual.

Availability: most good pet shops or even aquarists.

Longevity: can live to 20 years or more.

Sexual maturity: 3 years onwards.

Breeding: usually in late February when strings or masses of eggs are laid in watercourses such as ponds and lakes, with as many as 4000 eggs laid at any one time. They incubate in the water for about 2 weeks and then 'metamorphose', (hatch into tadpole and then grow their front and back legs, lose their tail and then come out onto the land as an adult miniature), in 2 months.

Caging: see chapter on amphibians. A purpose-built aquarium will cost around £15 ($22).

Diet: when at tadpole stage will eat vegetation such as algae, but will become carnivorous once adult, eating many forms of invertebrate such as flies, mealworms, earthworms etc. Feeding will cost about £1 per week, depending on how many animals are to be kept.

Diseases: see chapter on amphibians.

Comments: the common toad is the largest European toad and varies in size throughout its wide range. The females are normally larger than the males.

With its extremely warty skin, it is a very heavily built creature. It generally hides during the day in or under some damp vegetation. It uses the same place time after time and comes out at night to feed on various insects and other invertebrates. Toads hibernate during the winter months, and then can be seen congregating in very large numbers around February to March. They frequently return to the same water course each year where they lay thousands of eggs in thick jelly-like strings. These strings can exceed 25cm long. A very easy animal to keep and breed: keeping them in a pond would help in the breeding, as a small aquarium will not suffice for this purpose.

TORTOISE (Testudo graeca)

Distribution: world-wide in hot countries, such as Greece.

Cost and availability: the way tortoises were brought into this country in the 1980s and before was very distressing for them, and many were dead on arrival because of being stacked one on top of another. Some 300 animals could be packed into one small box by this method. Fortunately the law has changed, and the number of tortoises that any one pet shop or dealer can bring into this country in any one year has been dramatically reduced. Because of this, the price of the tortoise has risen, and the normal price for an average-sized animal is approximately £120 ($175).

Availability: from most good pet shops and some dealers.

Longevity: I have known of one specimen in Somerset which has been through two generations of owners, and is now over 120 years old. Average is around 100 years.

Size: this varies according to the species of tortoise, but for the 'common', over 30cm long.

Sexual maturity: can vary between 6 and 20 years.

Breeding: lays 6 to 10 eggs which are incubated for up to 120 days, but requires a temperature of 30°C (86°F).

Caging: see chapter on reptiles. Normally kept outdoors in the garden.

Diet: lettuce, dog food, cat food, carrot, cabbage, apple, dandelion leaves, grass etc. Feeding will cost about £2–3 per week as most items of food will be off-cuts of vegetables from the kitchen and dandelions from the garden.

Diseases: they are prone to getting abscesses, especially on the neck. Can also get insect larva infestation on the neck, which may look like an abscess. Consult your veterinary surgeon for advice before doing anything.

Comments: this particular species of tortoise has a slightly domed shell and a small spur on each of its front limbs. The females are generally larger than the males. They court in the spring, with the male biting and butting the female before mating her. The young tortoises are miniatures of the adults but their shells are rounder and the actual markings are much clearer.

These animals are a target for thieves, so good security in the garden is essential, especially at night, and ensure that your tortoise cannot escape through holes in the fencing.

13

KEEPING YOUR ANIMAL HEALTHY

HYGIENE AND DISEASE

When looking after any species of animal, keep hygienic conditions to a very high standard, so as not to allow any infection to breed within the enclosure or cage.

In the wild, infection is rare, as the build up of faecal droppings or unwanted food is minimal, and would normally be erased by the natural elements, or other animals in the food chain. The only time this breaks down is when animals scavenge food from human areas, e.g. refuse tips. This food, which has probably rotted and started to build up bacteria, can be eaten by wild animals and cause ailments such as food poisoning, which can eventually kill. This is more prevalent during the hotter months of the year, as bacteria thrive in warm weather.

Infection can easily be brought into the captive environment by wild bird droppings. The greenfinch, collared dove and wood pigeon are the worst culprits. Rats can also bring in disease, mainly in their urine, but this can be prevented by making the cage or enclosure 'rat proof'.

Inoculation of the captive animals can prevent such diseases as Pasteurella, which is part of the septicaemia group, one of which was known as the human plague.

Simple outbreaks of cold sores in humans can be spread to some animals, the monkey family in particular, with often fatal results. The marmoset and tamarin are the most vulnerable.

One disease that has been introduced by man, to control rabbits, is myxomatosis. It has spread continuously through the rabbit population, and many a poor animal can be seen suffering from this fatal illness. It is carried by fleas, and symptoms which show that a rabbit has it are inflammation of the eyes, anus, and other orifices, skin haemorrhages, and convulsions; usually death occurs within ten days. The only way to control it in pet rabbits is by vaccination. Any animal seen with the disease should be put down immediately, as it will be suffering immensely.

Fortunately, myxomatosis cannot be spread to any other species, so if a fox were to kill and eat an infected rabbit, it would have no effect on it.

A common infection in cage birds is Red Mite. These mites attack birds at night, and feed off their bodies. If serious infestations are allowed to continue without treatment, then anaemia (deficiency in the number of red blood cells) occurs, followed by death. Since the mites only attack at night, the birds need not be treated, but the cage should be completely disinfected during the day, whilst the birds are removed. The most common cause of infestation of Red Mite is insufficient cleaning of the cages, especially where perches come in contact with the walls.

Prevention is the best cure, and remember that all animals in captivity must have their food and water changed daily, to prevent bacteria from forming, and to keep them in top condition.

Cleaning of cages and enclosures is most important to keep down organisms which cause disease. These organisms are called pathogens: examples are, bacteria, viruses, and fungi. They are too small to see with the naked eye. Most can be spread in saliva, which may be on food, in bites, licking walls of cages and enclosures including the wire, utensils which may be used for cleaning (these should always be clean before use), and contaminated water. Bedding should be changed regularly.

Food also can be contaminated by flies, rodents or birds, if left in the cage too long.

Last but by no means least, YOU! can bring in disease on your hands, boots and clothing.

To prevent the spread of pathogens, wash the walls and floors of cages and enclosures daily with cold water. Your boots and hands should be washed with hot, soapy water.

When using any chemicals, proper concentrations must be adhered to, e.g. when using liquid detergent for cleaning feeding bowls and feeding areas, and these must be rinsed thoroughly with water after cleaning.

Some illnesses are transferable from animal to man. This is known as zoonosis. Below, I list a few of such illnesses, and what to look for.

a. Hepatitis, which is inflammation of the liver, can be found in the drop-pings of animals infected with a virus. In hepatitis A, the disease develops rapidly and is not usually severe; in hepatitis B, the disease takes longer to develop and can become chronic. Hepatitis can also be caused by (non-A) and (non-B) viruses.

b. Psittacosis is an infection passed on to humans by parrots. Primarily, it is contracted from the inhalation of contaminated dust, from the cage floor of a diseased bird. In humans the disease is similar to influenza, and has been known to be fatal.

c. Ringworm, which is a fungal infection, can affect humans on the head; on the legs (called Dhobies Itch); and on the feet (Athletes' Foot). On the skin, it takes the form of circular areas of dry scaling skin; and can be contracted from animals such as cattle, horses and domestic pets.

d. Salmonella, the bacteria which cause food-poisoning, can be passed to human food by the hands. Washing your hands after tending animals is most important to keep these bacteria at bay.

e. Tetanus, otherwise known as lockjaw, can be caused by not cleaning and covering cuts and other wounds properly, especially when working with animals or with the earth. The organism is present in the gut of animals, and droppings absorbed into the ground are a prominent source. The disease causes uncontrollable muscle contraction, firstly in the muscles in the neck and jaw, hence the alternative name lockjaw. In untreated cases, death from exhaustion occurs: therefore it is sensible to be inoculated regularly as a preventative.

Infections in humans are normally caused by dirty hands, cuts, sores and wounds. Always wash hands after working with your animals, never allow them to lick your face or mouth, never eat or use anything which has been soiled by them, and let your doctor know what animals you have.

PESTS AND PARASITES

Pests can come in all shapes and sizes, from the smallest insects, which may damage buildings or furnishings by tunnelling into the wood (woodworm), to human vandals. Other nuisances include rats, mice, moles, squirrels and rabbits, all of which do damage, and some can spread disease.

Some other pests are parasites. Parasites are organisms that cannot live an independent life, such as pathogens, fungi, lice, fleas, mites, ticks, worms and flukes. Lice, fleas, mites and ticks are ectoparasites, animals which live on the outside of other animals, the hosts. Worms and flukes are endoparasites, animals which live on the inside of other animals.

Ectoparasites which you may come across are:

a. Lice; these do not leave the host, as their eggs are laid in the hair or fur. The adults are normally found around the ears and the anus. Although they can be killed by dusting or bathing, the eggs cannot be killed on the first treatment, and after one week these begin to hatch, so a further treatment is needed then. There are now products on the market, which can be bought through the veterinary practices, that are applied only once and last for up to six months, thereby killing any further hatchings once the host has been sprayed.

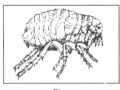

Flea

b. Fleas move around on the host in the hair or fur, and lay their eggs, which then fall to the ground. These will not hatch into fleas unless they are vibrated, e.g. by a passing animal, onto which they will then jump. They can be killed in the same way as the lice.

c. Mites have four pair of legs, and burrow into the skin of the host they live on. They eat skin flakes and blood, which creates sores, scabies, mange and scaly leg on birds. The only treatment is isolation and disinfestation of both the host animal, and its cage or enclosure. Repeat after one week.

d. Ticks insert their heads into the skin of the host, and suck the blood. They need only feed once before dropping their eggs on the ground. The only treatment is to kill and remove the tick, making sure the head is taken out from the host's body, as leaving it behind can cause infection.

The only endoparasite I shall mention is the roundworm. Infestation with roundworm can cause blindness. Young animals (5–8 weeks old) are more vulnerable to roundworm than adults.

This worm lives in the intestine, and its eggs are passed out in the host's droppings. These eggs are then picked up from the ground by other animals, then swallowed. In the intestine they hatch into larvae, and invade the hepatic portal vein, which is in the liver, and the lungs. Then as they grow, they move from the liver and the lungs, back into the animal's mouth where they are swallowed once more into the intestine to become adult, and lay more eggs.

The life cycle takes about 4 weeks, and the adult worm reaches 10cm in length. To control roundworm, good hygiene is always essential. Any new animals should be isolated and droppings tested for eggs, and regular worming should be carried out where necessary. Human children can also become infected.

N.B. ALWAYS CONSULT A VETERINARY SURGEON BEFORE ATTEMPTING ANY TREATMENT.

ANIMAL FIRST AID

Animal first aid really means the form of treatment that can be given, until a full diagnosis and professional treatment can be administered by a veterinary surgeon.

First aid treatment can be to alleviate shock, relieve pain, and preserve the health of the animal, and sometimes simply means leaving it alone.

When an animal shows signs of illness, always note the time of onset, listing the peculiarities, so as to give as much information as possible to the vet.

Circumstances which may involve first aid are as follows:

a. An accident to the animal: e.g. a fall
b. A wound: e.g. a cut, possibly created by the above
c. A bite: e.g. inflicted by a cage mate or by itself
d. A heart attack: brought on by stress, or maybe disease
e. Poisoning: from food left in the cage for too long, or maybe contracted from wild birds or rodents

f. A choking fit: getting a bone lodged in the throat
g. A fit: loss of consciousness, or possible epilepsy
h. An animal giving birth: e.g. a mammal having difficulty in passing the youngster

Types of first aid to be given may include:

1. Removing the cause of the injury, such as a piece of glass
2. Trying to stop the bleeding, by pressure over the wound
3. Relieving interference in breathing: try to dislodge the object
4. Covering any wound with a clean temporary dressing, by using a towel or bandage
5. Separation from any other animals, putting the ill animal into a separate cage

Keep the animal warm at all times, and speak to it calmly using its name, giving as much TLC (tender loving care) as possible. Try to give the animal complete privacy, away from other people.

CALL THE VETERINARY SURGEON.

PETS IN NEED OF VETS

You may know that your pet needs a vet, but realise that veterinary bills are expensive and that you may not be able to afford them.

If you or your family are British rent payers who receive Housing Benefit, or home owners/mortgage payers receiving Council Tax benefit, then you qualify for free treatment from the PDSA.

The PDSA (People's Dispensary for Sick Animals) run 45 PetAid hospitals in major towns and cities, treating over 1.3 million cases annually, and a further 90 communities benefit from PetAid practices, a service which operates through participating private veterinary practices.

Ninety per cent of all animals given this free treatment are dogs and cats, many of which are road accident victims. The service is funded by legacies, donations and fundraising activites. The PDSA is always keen to hear from volunteers willing to help. See the list of useful contacts at the end of this book.

GENERAL FEEDING

To keep animals healthy, we try to bear certain things in mind.

Firstly, the behaviour of an animal in captivity can be dictated by the type of environment we can afford to give it, so we should try to ensure that its environment is beneficial.

Secondly, it is important that this environment is kept clean and free from disease, so that the animals within it are healthy and fit.

Thirdly, we must always ensure that the animal is offered good wholesome foodstuffs, and to observe that it is feeding well.

To keep animals successfully, we must know and understand what they would eat in the wild, and how that food is obtained. Then, try to give each animal plenty of opportunity to carry out its natural instincts; allow it to 'search and find', instead of just putting food on a plate. This we call animal 'enrichment', which in turn reduces the possibility of stereotypical problems, which can be detrimental.

The storage of foodstuffs is important, as the presentation of food is influential to the well being of the animal. Therefore they should be kept dry, away from rodents, and used within their individual time limits.

To determine whether an animal is well fed, we should firstly look at its condition. Should the normal animal be thin or fat? See if the hair/fur or feathers are sleek and well groomed, if the animal has bright eyes, if it is active and alert, and enjoys its food and if its droppings are normal. Is its behaviour normal, and can it reproduce?

All animals on this earth require the same food chemicals.

Organic chemicals
a) Proteins, which are broken down into amino acids, are required to build up body structures and membranes.
b) Carbohydrates are needed as a source of energy for the body.
c) Saturated fats, which can be made in the body of the animal from sugar, are also required as a source of energy.
d) Unsaturated fats, which are obtained in food either from plants or meat.
e) Vitamins, which are chemicals found in foodstuffs.

Inorganic chemicals

a) Salts, which are chemicals in foods and, like vitamins, do not have to be digested before absorption into the body.
b) Water, which is 'eaten' as part of all foods and is also drunk, makes up much of the fluid in an animal's body; enough must be taken daily to make up for the loss of water in its normal bodily functions.
c) Minerals are needed in small amounts for the chemical activity in the animal's body, and for making body structures.

Natural foods that can be given to animals consist of fresh fruits, fresh vegetables, meats, nuts, seeds, fish, grains etc. In captivity, bread is also used for roughage, as already stated, and because many animals enjoy it. Artificial foods are also given as these are made from natural foods, but are processed so as to also contain food chemicals. These foods are easy to store and also easy to give, although most animals prefer natural fresh foods.

The types of natural foods given to animals depends on what they would consume in the wild, and whether those foods are available and can be provided, and whether we can allow the animal to deal with the food as it would in the wild.

When looking at natural foods, we can separate them into two groups, the plants and the animals. Plant food can then be divided into four different groups.

1. Shrubs and trees. Suitable foods for deer etc.
2. Herbs and grasses. Suitable foods for sheep etc.
3. Fruits and seeds. Suitable foods for birds and some mammals etc.
4. Nectar and sap which are found in flowers (nectar) and under the bark of trees (saps). Suitable foods for monkeys and birds etc.

Animal food can be divided into six groups.

1. Invertebrates – insects etc. Suitable foods for most other animals.
2. Small vertebrates – mice etc. Suitable foods for reptiles, owls, and carnivorous mammals etc.
3. Large vertebrates – deer etc. Suitable foods for lions, bears etc.
4. Blood – drunk mainly by vampire bats.

5. Eggs – these may come from birds or some reptiles. Suitable foods for other birds, some reptiles, mammals etc.
6. Milk – comes from the mammary glands of mammals, for feeding to young, and of course milk from cows for human consumption.

Substitute foods consist of plant fibre. This may be in the form of hay, straw, clover, and dried leaves which are suitable foods for cattle, sheep etc.

Compound substitute foods, otherwise known as concentrates, use products such as oats, barley, wheat, bran, yeast, bonemeal, milk powder, salt and vitamins. These come in cake form or pellet form. With these dry foodstuffs, animals can become bored, as there is no element of surprise in eating them.

Last but not least come the supplements. These are additives, usually in powder form, which give extra food chemicals such as trace elements and vitamins.

Vitamins

Because vitamins behave like catalysts, they are only required in small amounts. Some vitamins are excreted from the body very quickly. Therefore, they need to be replaced frequently from foodstuffs. Other, 'fat-soluble' vitamins can be stored in the body for several months.

Fat-Soluble Vitamins

VITAMIN 'A'   This does not occur in plants, but its forerunner 'carotene' does. This can be converted to vitamin A within the alimentary tract. Carotene is found in green leafy materials, but grains, roots and tubers are poor sources except for carrots. Halibut and cod-liver oils are rich in vitamin A. This vitamin is quickly absorbed and stored in the liver. Outside the body, vitamin A and carotene are easily destroyed when exposed to air and light.

Vitamin A is required for the eyes, skin, bones, and reproductive organs, and it has been observed that blindness and deafness can be caused by its lack.

VITAMIN 'D' This is absent from many natural foodstuffs. The only rich source is cod-liver oil. Ultra violet rays from the sun produce vitamin 'D' from precursors which are present in the skin and some glands of the animal. Sun-cured, soft, green leafy hays have a higher vitamin 'D' content than pale-stemmed hays.

Vitamin 'D' is stored in the body, but to a lesser extent than vitamin 'A'.

It is required, together with calcium and phosphorus, for the normal growth of bone. Rickets is a disease associated with abnormal bone growth, and can arise from the deficiency of calcium in the absence of vitamin 'D'. Such bone as is formed is weak and mishapen. Tension from the muscles can pull the bones out of shape, then the actual body weight will bend the leg bones, which in turn may fracture. The requirement for vitamin 'D', calcium and phosphorus is greater when growth is rapid, in youth and during pregnancy and lactation.

VITAMIN 'E' This is found mostly in wheat-germ oil, although whole cereal grains and green leafy materials are also good sources. Vitamin 'E' is stored in the animal's body for long periods. The precise function of this vitamin has not yet been fully determined, although we do know that it is important for normal reproduction, to prevent muscular weaknesses, and to prevent paralysis. Because there is a wide distribution of this vitamin in many foodstuffs, its deficiency is very uncommon.

VITAMIN 'K' This is found in green leafy materials, although, in mammals, micro-organisms present in the intestines synthesise sufficient vitamin 'K' to supply their needs. Birds are really the only creatures which require this vitamin in their food. Its lack can create an increase in the clotting time of blood. Therefore, haemorrhages occur in the skin and the muscles.

Water-Soluble Vitamins

VITAMIN 'C' Only monkeys, humans and guinea pigs require a dietary source of this vitamin, as other species have the ability to synthesise it within their own bodies.

Vitamin 'C' can be found in large quantities in green leafy materials, citrus fruits, tomatoes, and potatoes.

The animal body has little resource to store this vitamin, so it must be supplied continuously in the diet. Stored foods quickly lose their vitamin 'C' content, and cooking destroys it.

This vitamin is important in the intercellular material in soft tissue and bone. If there is a breakdown in the intercellular material, the bones may become weak and easily fracture. Gums may swell and bleed, and the teeth loosen. The walls of small blood vessels may rupture allowing the escape of blood into surrounding tissues, causing haemorrhages throughout the body. Scurvy is the name given to the disease associated with the lack of this vitamin.

VITAMIN 'B' COMPLEX This complex is made up of aneurin (vitamin 'B1', thiamine), riboflavin (vitamin 'B2', vitamin 'G') nicotinic acid, pantothenic acid, pyridoxine (vitamin 'B6'), p-aminobenzoic acid, biotin, folic acid, cyanocobalamin (vitamin 'B12') and inositol. All are responsible for the breakdown and rebuilding of the digested and absorbed components of foodstuffs, creating energy for the animal, and for new tissue to be laid down and existing tissue maintained.

Deficiency is not usually isolated to one of the 'B' vitamins; it has normally a multiple cause, and may result in loss of weight, loss of appetite, apathy (lack of emotion), skin lesions, anaemia, loss and/or greying of hair. Beri-beri in man has been recorded as caused by lack of this complex, as has pellagra (black-tongue in the dog) through a deficiency in nicotinic acid. Symptoms of black-tongue are mouth ulcers, halitosis and loss of appetite, with bad discoloration of the tongue.

'B' vitamins can be found in liver, yeast, the germ and outer husks of cereals, green leafy materials and milk.

No 'B' vitamin is stored in an animal's body for long periods, so, like vitamin 'C', they have to be supplied on a regular basis from the diet.

TABLE OF CAGE SIZES

These sizes are at minimum: wherever possible give as much room as is practicable.

Cage bird (budgerigar or canary)	Normal bird cage bought from any pet shop.
Cage bird (parrot)	Parrot cage from pet shop for small parrot up to the size of an African grey but in the case of a macaw a large aviary should be provided. Minimum size 2m high by 2m deep and 4m long.
Vivarium (small snake or lizard)	A 1m aquarium with secure ventilated lid.
Vivarium (large snake e.g. Boa)	The snake will grow up to 5-6m long so naturally the larger the cage the better. Minimum is 6-7m long by 2m wide and 2m high.
Aquarium (freshwater)	5 litres of water to every 12.5 mm of fish.
Aquarium (salt water)	A minimum of 100 litres capacity will dictate the size of your aquarium.
Tarantula	These require very little room so a small aquarium with a secure ventilated lid is sufficient.
Terrarium (single species)	A small aquarium with a secure ventlated lid.
Terrarium (mixed collection)	4–6 small amphibians will need a 1–2m aquarium at minimum.

Rabbit	Ready made hutch from any pet stores, but offer the animal a secure wire run with a roof to deter predators, which can be placed on the grass.
Guinea pig	As for the rabbit.
Mice (one pair)	Minimum 60cm long by 23cm deep by 23cm high.
Rats (one pair)	Minimum 1m long by 30cm deep by 30cm high.
Marmoset (one pair indoors)	2m high by 1.2m deep and 1.2m wide is the bare minimum
Marmoset (potential breeding pair, outdoors)	Minimum 2m high by 2m deep and 2m long main enclosure, with a 2m high by 2m deep by 2m long internal cage with sufficient heating and double doors. (See diagram under chapter on Marmosets and Tamarins, p.89.)
Chinchilla (single animal)	A tall cage 2m high by 1m deep and 1m wide. If keeping a pair then double up on the width and depth.
Siberian chipmunk (one pair)	Minimum 1.2m long by 1m deep by 2m high.

14
REFERENCES

Hershkovitz P. (1977)   *Living New World Monkeys*
                        University of Chicago Press.

Fisher, Lady   *Hand-rearing Marmosets and Tamarins*
                        from Kilverstone Wildlife Park, Thetford, Norfolk.

Kleiman D. (1977)   *The Biology and Conservation of the Callitrichidae*
                        Smithsonian Institution Press, Washington, DC.

Moore M. (1989)   *Marmosets in Captivity*
                        Bassett Publications, Plymouth.

Gillette E. (1988)   *Chipmunks in Captivity*
                        Bassett Publications, Plymouth.

Dept. of Education   London

The Cincinnati Zoo,   3400 Vine Street, Cincinnati, Ohio 45220

15

PRODUCTS MENTIONED IN THE TEXT

* ABIDEC multivitamin – Warner Lambert Health Centre, Mitchell House, Southampton Road, Eastleigh, Hants SO5 5RY

* Cytacon B12 – Duncan Flockhart and Co. Ltd., 700 Oldfield Lane North, Greenford, Middlesex UB6 0HD

* Milupa Infant Food – Milupa Ltd., Milupa House, Uxbridge Road, Hillingdon, Uxbridge, Middlesex UB10 9NA

† SA37 Vitamin Powder – Intervet UK Ltd., Science Park, Milton Road, Cambridge, CB4 4FP

* SMA Powdered Human Milk Substitute – John Wyeth and Brothers Ltd., Wyeth Laboratories, Huntercombe Lane South, Taplow, Maidenhead, Berks SL6 0PH

• Vitamin D3 – Roche Products Ltd., P.O. Box 8, Welwyn Garden City, Herts AL7 3AY

CATAC feeding bottles – Catac Products Ltd., Catac House, 1 Newnham Street, Bedford MK40 3JR (available direct or through larger pet shops)

MARMOSET JELLY – Special Diets Services, PO Box 705, Witham, Essex CM8 3AD (available from SDS only)

* Available from pharmacists
• Available from/through your veterinary surgeon
† Available from pet shops or your veterinary surgeon

16
FURTHER READING

A Manual of the Care and Treatment of Children's and Exotic Pets, edited by A.F. Cowie, British Small Animal Veterinary Association, 7 Mansfield Street, London W1M 0AT

Dodo, The Scientific Journal of Jersey Wildlife Preservation Trust, Les Augres Manor, Jersey, C.I.

International Zoo Yearbooks, edited by P.J.S. Olney, published by The Zoological Society of London, Regent's Park, NW1 4RY

Proceedings of Symposia of the Association of British Wild Animal Keepers, Bristol Zoo, Bristol.

Black's Veterinary Dictionary, published by A & C Black Ltd., Alderman House, 37 Soho Square, London, W1D 3QZ.

17

LIST OF USEFUL CONTACTS

In the UK

Animals and You
D.C. Thomson & Co. Ltd.
185 Fleet Street
London
EC4A 2HS

Animal Welfare
UFAW
The Old School House
Brewhouse Hill
Wheathampstead
St Albans
AL4 8AN

Association of British Wild Animal
    Keepers
ABWAK
12 Tackley Road
Eastville
Bristol
BS5 6UQ

BBC Wildlife Magazine
BBC Broadcasting House
Whiteladies Road
Bristol
BS8 2LR

Bird Keeper
IPC Magazines
Specialist Magazine Group
Kings Reach Tower
Stamford Street
London
SE1 9LS

Born Free Foundation
3 Grove House
Foundry Lane
Horsham
West Sussex
RH13 5PL

British Trust for Ornithology
Newell House
Winkfield
Windsor
Berkshire
SL4 4SE

Budgerigar World Ltd.
County Press Buildings
Bala
Gwynedd LL23 7PG
Wales

Care for the Wild
Ashfolds
Rusper
Horsham
West Sussex
RH12 4QX

Cats Protection League
PO Box 314
Horsham
West Sussex
RH13 5FE

Cat World Ltd.
Avalon Court
Star Road
Partridge Green
West Sussex
RH13 8RY

Dog World & *Dog World Annual*
M. J. Boulding
Editor and Publisher
9 Tufton Street
Ashford
Kent
TN23 1QN

Dogs Monthly
RTC Associates
Ascot House
High Street
Ascot
Berkshire
SL5 7JG

Dogs Today
Pet Subjects Ltd.
Pankhurst Farm
Bagshot Road
West End
Nr. Woking
Surrey
GU24 9QR

International Council for Bird
    Preservation
32 Cambridge Road
Girton
Cambridge
CB3 0PJ

Kennel and Cattery Management
Albatross Publications
PO Box 193
Dorking
Surrey
RH5 5YF

Kennel Club Yearbook
Kennel Club
1 Clarges Street
London
W1Y 8AB

New Scientist
Holborn Publishing Group
Kings Reach Tower
Stamford Street
London
SE1 9LS

Our Dogs Publishing Co.Ltd.
5 James Leigh Street
Manchester
M1 6EX

PDSA
Whitechapel Way
Priorslee
Telford
Shropshire
TF2 9PQ

Racing Pigeon Pictorial
Racing Pigeon Publishing Co. Ltd.
13 Guilford Street
London
WC1N 1DX

RSPCA
The Causeway
Horsham
West Sussex
RH12 1HG

The National Council for
  Aviculture
Gardeners Cottage
Williamscot
Oxon
OX17 1AD

The Ridgeway Trust for
  Endangered Cats
7 Parkwood Road
Hastings
East Sussex
TN34 2RN

Southern Aviaries
Tinkers' Lane
Hadlow Down
Uckfield
Sussex
TN22 4EU

You & Your Vet
British Veterinary Association
7 Mansfield Street
London
W1M 0AT

In Europe

Aquarium Magazine
Editions du Garou
5 Rue Thiergarten
67000 Strasbourg
France

Pets Europe
InterMedium Publishers
PO Box 1176
3600 BD Maarssen
Netherlands

The Americas

Animal Town News
Killian Graphics
Box 91
Chatham NJ 07928
USA

Cockatiel and Parrot World
850 Park Avenue
Monterey
CA 93940
USA

International Ferret Review
Ferret Fanciers Club
711 Chautauqua Ct.
Pittsburgh
PA 15214
USA

Pets Quarterly Magazine
151-8333 Jones Road
Richmond
BC V6Y 1L5
Canada

Poodle Review
Hoflin Publishing Ltd.
4401 Zephyr Street
Wheat Ridge
CO 80033
USA

Pot Bellied Pigs
Sarnan Publications
Box 768
Pleasant Grove
CA 95668
USA

Rare Breeds Journal
Box 66
Crawford
NE 69339
USA

Reptile and Amphibian Magazine
1168 Rte. 61, S.,
Pottsville
PA 17901
USA

Rest of World

Australian Canary Breeder
Canary Breeders Association of
    Australia
13 Robina Road
Eaglemont
Victoria 3084
Australia

Pet World
Ikebukuro Nishiguchi Sky Building
2-14-4 Ikebukuro
Toshima-ku
Tokyo 171
Japan
(The only magazine of the pet
    industry in Japan)

INDEX